From Babe To Son- A 40-Day Discipleship Devotional

Cheptoo Morei

Published by Cheptoo Morei, 2024.

FROM BABE TO SON- A 40-DAY DISCIPLESHIP DEVOTIONAL

First edition. March 26, 2024.

ISBN: 979-8224465101

Written by Cheptoo Morei.

Also by Cheptoo Morei

Abraham's Seed
From Babe To Son- A 40-Day Discipleship Devotional

Why Should You Read This Book?

In the realm of Biblical numerology, the number forty carries profound significance, symbolizing a period of testing and transformation. Throughout the Bible, great figures embarked on 40-day fasts, emerging with newfound spiritual power, revelation, and wisdom to fulfill their divine callings.

Consider Moses, who, after a 40-day fast, inscribed the Ten Commandments and received divine guidance for the people of Israel. Reflect on Elijah, who, following his 40-day fast, received prophetic insights into the destiny of Israel. And of course, contemplate Jesus, who, after fasting for 40 days, was imbued with the authority and anointing that ushered in the era of the New Testament.

Fasting, the act of denying oneself physical sustenance, is not merely about abstaining from food—it's a conduit for revelation, which flows from a deep immersion in the Word of God. Thus, this study presents itself as a 40-day Word Fast, tailored for those new to the faith (spiritual infants) who crave the nourishment of God's Word as essential sustenance for their souls.

During these forty days, commit at least thirty minutes to studying a chapter of the Bible, allowing its teachings to permeate your being. Then, spend an additional thirty minutes meditating on the day's lesson, engraving it upon your heart for lasting transformation.

The **40-Day Discipleship Devotional** serves as a cornerstone, laying a doctrinal foundation by imparting the core tenets of the gospel. Recognizing the value of repetition in learning, revisit this devotional every three months, reinforcing your understanding until your spiritual foundation is unshakable.

With humility and sincerity, I offer this treasury of wisdom to you, dear reader. May each study ignite a flame of faith within you, empowering you to effect profound change in your life and circumstances.

Without Wax,
Cheptoo Morei.

Introduction

I recently had a profound realization that shook the very foundation of my beliefs: "Faith without Works is dead." It's like the divine choreography of creation itself - when God sculpted man and woman in His image and likeness, it wasn't just a passive act. He intricately formed them from the very earth, breathing life into their beings. Faith, I've come to understand, is the potent force behind creation, while works are the tangible manifestation of that belief. We don't pray to receive; we pray because we've already received. We don't work to earn; we receive so we can work. It's a beautiful synergy between the spiritual and the physical.

Think about it - the spirit grasps the wisdom of God, the soul directs the body, and the body carries out the actions. It's a holistic process, requiring alignment of body, mind, and spirit. And where does it all begin? With faith. As Romans 10:17 reminds us, faith comes by hearing the word of God. That's why delving into the Scriptures isn't just about acquiring knowledge; it's about igniting that spark of faith within us.

Proverbs 24:3-4 paints a vivid picture of the richness that comes from wisdom, understanding, and knowledge. Studying the word of God isn't just an academic exercise - it's about cultivating a receptive heart, and nurturing a faith that can move mountains.

So, here's the purpose of this devotional journey: to immerse you in the Word, to fine-tune your spiritual ears until faith resonates deep within you. It's about nurturing your relationship with Christ, anchoring you so securely in your faith that nothing in this world can shake you.

Joshua 6- Strength to Will, Courage to Do.

Jericho stood fortified, a symbol of strength and security, yet it trembled under the looming presence of the Israelites. Fear gripped the hearts of its king and valiant defenders at the very sight of the children of Israel encamped nearby.

Joshua 6:1 "Now Jericho was straitly shut up because of the children of Israel; none went out, and none came in."

The city was under siege for a reason – the Lord had already declared it as the inheritance of Israel. All they needed to do was step forward in faith and claim what was promised. With God on their side, a plan was already set in motion. (Exodus 19:5, 34:9, Leviticus 26:12)

The how (Joshua 6:3-5)

We continue to observe and marvel at the faithfulness and courage of Joshua as the leader. Even in this, he did exactly as the Lord commanded. In verse 10, he commanded the people not to make a noise or even speak a word until he bade them to. In future studies, we shall get an opportunity to explore the importance of silence when God is working.

We also observe that every day as they did the march, early in the morning, they maintained the ordered formation.

"Shout! For the Lord hath given you the city." Was the call they were all anticipating on each of the six days they went out at dawn to compass the city. Finally, on the seventh day, as the Lord's work was perfected, the call came, the people shouted and the walls came down.

Before they could shout and possess, the Lord gave them further instructions.

***Joshua 6:17-19** "And the city shall be accursed, even it, and all that are therein, to the Lord: only Rahab the harlot shall live, she and all that are with her in the house, because she hid the messengers that we sent. And ye, in any wise keep yourselves from the accursed thing, lest ye make yourselves accursed, when ye take of the accursed thing, and make the camp of Israel a curse, and trouble it. But all the silver, and gold, and vessels of brass and iron, are consecrated unto the Lord: they shall come into the treasury of the Lord."*

For the six days that they marched, they had all the tools they needed to take Jericho; the priests were blowing the ram horns, the Ark of God was with them and they had an army. But it was not yet time. God was still working, every day they needed to march as a declaration of faith. When the Lord says *'be patient'*, He does not mean sit on your hands and do nothing, He means *'do as I told you to do, every day without fail, wait in expectation. Express your faith and trust every day in doing what you have been called to do in this season as you hope and wait for the one that I am getting ready for you.'*

I can imagine that every day when the children of Israel marched around the city, it sounded like a great army to those within. Each morning when they heard the ram horns being blown, they anticipated an attack. When the walls came down, the people of Jericho were already defeated in spirit.

The city was accursed in the eyes of God. They burned it down to the ground, to cleanse the land and prevent temptation.

So the Lord was with Joshua, and his fame was noised throughout all the country. Why? Because he feared the Lord, (Joshua 1:8), he had the strength of will the Lord's will, and the courage to do the Lord's will.

A willing heart makes a strong mind which then becomes courageous enough to command the body to do.

"Be ye doers of the word, and not hearers only, deceiving your selves." -James 1:22.

" For not hearers of the law are just before God, but the doers of the law shall be justified.- Romans 2:13.

"Therefore whosoever heareth these sayings of mine, and doeth them, I will liken him unto a wise man, which built his house upon a rock: And the rain descended, and the floods came, and the winds blew, and beat upon that house; and it fell not: for it was founded upon a rock."- Matthew 7:24,25.

Titus 3- Maintain Good Works.

From the previous study, we have learned that doing is part of believing. Whether it is dwelling in prayer or performing a physical activity, works give expression to our faith. Now let us look at how we are to act while performing the acts of faith.

Titus was a letter of Paul to Titus, then the bishop/overseer of the church of the Cretians. As is the basic structure of letters, it begins with a salutation and ends with one.

The main topics of discussion in this chapter are our attitude and conduct towards secular authority, our fellow man, our brothers and sisters in Christ, and the church as an institution.

It begins in Verse 1 with how to conduct ourselves towards the government of the day. The **attitude** we are encouraged to adopt is one of subjection/submission. This should come easy to us as the Bible tells us all powers on earth are God-sanctioned; the extension being that we are not to complain about but pray for the institutions. Our **conduct** should be of positive active participation where called to. The modern-day translation is: "Pay your taxes, obey the law, work diligently, pray for your country..." just to mention a few.

Towards fellow man, we should **put on the garment** of gentleness and **show it off** with meekness unto all. (v.2)

The Bible also reminds us that we all were: foolish, disobedient, deceived, serving diverse lusts and pleasures, living in malice and envy, hateful, and hating one another before the Lord came on the scene, and according to His mercy *saved us, made us anew* and *is constantly renewing* us by the Holy Ghost is us. (v.4-7) By the way, if the above list does not resonate with the old you, you might need deliverance from deception and denial.

There is an exhortation in v.3 to constantly affirm to each other the fact expressed in V.7:

"That being justified by His grace, we should be made heirs according to the hope of eternal life."

After all, one of the reasons for pursuing holiness in our Christian living is because we know and believe that Jesus is coming back.

V.8

"... that they which have believed in God might be careful to maintain good works."

We are reminded to avoid *trivialities* that could lead to division and confusion.

The command on dealing with <u>an unrepentant saint</u> is quite clear and succinct, after the first and second corrections, REJECT, without feeling guilty because they condemned themselves for their actions.

The letter ends poetically with a salutation, and instruction, as of a shepherd to his sheep, an apostle to his flock in the faith. It is a reminder to care for each other materially as part of the body.

It would be unfinished if Paul hadn't added, as a reminder to the church, his *'for those who maybe weren't listening to the letter, hear this.'*

V.14

"And let ours also learn to maintain good works for necessary uses, that they be not unfruitful."

You cannot produce good fruit unless you are dedicated to good works, and you cannot produce much fruit and fruit that remains if you do not maintain good works. And finally, if you are not doing good works, you are doing dead works.

From this text, good works are: being submitted to authority, helping the poor and needy, being kind and gentle with all people, working hard for your material and spiritual growth, and staying away from company that corrupts the gift of salvation in you.

"And now also the axe is laid unto the root of the trees: therefore every tree which bringeth not forth good fruit is hewn down, and cast into the fire."- Matthew 3:10

"Even so every good tree bringeth forth good fruit, but a corrupt tree bringeth forth evil fruit. A good tree cannot bring forth evil fruit, neither can a corrupt tree bring forth good fruit. Every tree that bringeth not forth good fruit is hewn down, and cast into the fire." -Matthew 7:17-19

" I am the vine, ye are the branches: He that abideth in me, and I in him, the same bringeth forth much fruit: for without me ye can do nothing."- John 15:5

"Ye have not chosen me, but I have chosen you, and ordained you, that ye should go and bring forth fruit, and that your fruit should remain: that whatsoever ye shall ask of the Father in my name, he may give it you."- John 15:16

Genesis 3- Doubt, Disbelieve, Disobey.

" *For we walk by faith, not by sight:*"- 2nd Corinthians 5:7

I once heard someone say "The only thing satan has is a big mouth and millennia of experience.", I agree with the statement. Any time you get into a verbal/mental exchange with the devil, be aware that he is cleverer than you and only Jesus can help.

"Now the serpent was more subtil(cunning/shrewd) than any beast of the field which the Lord God had made."- Genesis 3:1

The devil had taken the physical form of a snake and gone to the Garden of Eden to corrupt and usurp. His goal to steal, kill, and destroy, did not begin in the times of Jesus' sojourn on earth. I dare submit that his masterpiece was on this day in the garden.

Notice that he did not begin with a statement, but a question. He led Eve into sin, he did not force her into it as that would be in direct violation of the God-ordained gift of free will to all creation. And the woman, perhaps out of curiosity or boredom, answered the serpent in verse 3:

"God hath said, Ye shall not eat it, neither shall ye touch it, lest ye die."

At this juncture, I usually imagine in my mind that the serpent's eyes glistened and darted naughtily as he licked his lips in excitement before presenting his antithesis, '*You shall not surely die God is denying you an opportunity to be almost like Him and be independent of Him. To know yourself and therefore decide for yourself!*'(Proverbs 15:2). He told her that eating the fruit would make them divine beings/gods, knowing good and bad. Up to that point, Adam and Eve lived and did things but they could not condemn themselves of any sin because they did not know good and evil (Romans 3:20, 4:15). They had been living under the grace/covering of God, in a state where they lived only to do His will. The serpent knew that the only way to make them guilty of sin was to convince them to reject grace and take up the law, which in its integrity defines good and evil and the consequences for acting for or against one or the other.

At that moment, Eve began walking by sight rather than faith. Sight is our senses, the flesh, and when we are led by them we are no longer being led by the spirit, and the result is 1st John 2:16.

"And when the woman saw that the tree was good for food (lust of the flesh), and that it was pleasant to the eyes (lust of the eyes), and that it was desired to make one wise (pride of life), she took of the fruit thereof, and did eat, and gave also unto her husband with her, and he did eat." *- **Genesis 3:6***

Once you doubt, and then disbelieve, the action of disobedience becomes almost like an involuntary impulse. **A heart without God doesn't struggle to birth sin.** Between verses six and seven their spiritual disconnection happened, their souls were corrupted with rebellion and their physical decay began.

Why did they hide from God? Because they were naked, afraid, and ashamed. Satan led them into iniquity and corrupted their nature. He introduced into them a voice almost, that accused them of wrong and condemned them of their sin, and it became common for all mankind from then on. All the law does is turn your eyes from Christ to you, and make you aware of your nakedness. Any belief or stronghold that turns your attention from God to you, and tries to convince you that you can do it, that your works can qualify you is only making you realize how naked you are. Nobody can fulfill the whole law, it is why we need grace, and we need to be veiled with the righteousness of Christ.

Notice that, unlike the serpent, God did respect the ordained order, all the instructions and questions were communicated to Adam who was the higher authority, who then communicated to Eve and together they would execute. Satan spoke to the uncovered woman.

The consequences that followed their breaking of the agreement were as follows:

The serpent- would walk on his belly and eat dirt forever. There would be enmity between him and the woman and between his seed and the woman's seed. And he would strike at his heel, and the human would strike at his head.

The woman- would experience the pain of reproduction, like cramps and pain in childbirth. Her desire would be for her husband and he would rule over her (1st Corinthians 4:35, 7:34).

The man- the ground was cursed for his sake, he would have to toil to harvest. Thorns, thistles, and weeds were to be born out of the ground to make his work even harder.

And finally, physical decay and death became the inheritance of all the descendants of Adam.

In verse 20, the concept of ancestry is introduced, and Adam finally named his wife Eve, the mother of all.

Because our God is merciful, the first sacrifice was offered. An animal died so that Adam and Eve could be clothed/covered, the same way Jesus Christ the Passover lamb was offered so that we could be clothed in His righteousness. (V.21)

The chapter ends sadly for humanity, in V.24:

"So He drove out the man, and placed at the east of the garden of Eden a cherubim, and a flaming sword which turned every way, to keep the way of the tree of life."

Thank God for His sacrifice, because there is hope for us yet... Revelation 22:2, 22:14. We who overcome shall be allowed back in to dwell with Christ in eternity.

Until then dear pilgrim, be like Jesus and not like Eve, when the enemy tries to tempt you, pull out the sword of the Spirit and proclaim IT IS WRITTEN! (Matthew 4:1-11)

Job 9- How can Man be Just before God?

Job speaks in hopeless surrender, in his depressed estate. He speaks of the majesty and the unexplainable and immeasurable power of the Lord God, juxtaposed against the wretchedness and weakness of man.

The summary of what he was trying to express is that he did not understand why he was going through all he had to go through, but that God did and that He alone could make it abate. In verse 2 he expressly says that man cannot win a suit against God.

There is also an air of self-righteous sentiment in Job, which he expresses in verses 16 and 17 when he supposes that he was inflicted without cause. Let us begin by exploring the power and majesty of the Almighty God:

★ If He spoke 1000 words men could not fault one. (v.3)

★ He holds all wisdom and strength (v.4)

★ No creature ever challenged Him and came out whole (v.4)

★ Our prosperity and success depends on Him(v.4)

★ He uproots the mountains and plants them at will. (v.5)

★ He can shake the earth off its foundations and break the pillars that support it. (v.6)

★ He can command the sun not to rise and can destroy the stars. (v.7)

★ He made the firmament and walked on the back of the sea until it took form. (v.8)

★ He made all the stars and knows them by name. (v.9)

★ He does great things, beyond which we can imagine or discover. (v.10)

★ He is Spirit, we cannot see Him, He is omnipresent. (v.11)

★ He gives and takes as He pleases, He is answerable to no one. (v.12)

★ When He is angry, all powers, beings, and principalities tremble. (v.13)

★ In a contest of strength, He is stronger than all. (v.19)

★ In a contest of law, He is the great judge. (v.19)

Wretched man on the other hand:

❖ Is unrighteous, unjust, unholy, and imperfect before God. (v.20)

❖ Does not truly know himself and has a naturally corrupt soul. (v.21)

❖ Is powerless and inconsequential in comparison to God. (v.22)

❖ His days are swifter than a post. (a messenger on foot), life is short and physical death is certain. (v.25, 26)

❖ Is judged guilty in God's eyes, if He is judged based on his person. (v.28)

❖ Is wicked. (v.29)

❖ Is not capable of being cleansed, justified, or made righteous of his power. (v.30,31).

❖ There's no person/being that can judge God or negotiate with God as equals. (v.32,33)

We cannot fault Job, seeing as we are as human as he was, and in some ways maybe he was better than we are. We can only thank God that while he lived in the age of law and judgement, we live in the age of grace. Job's final statement in verses 34 and 35 reminds us that without God's mercy, we are perished.

His discourse did not end there, but ours does for today, only I leave you with one question:

How can a man be righteous before God? (V.2)

Romans 4- Faith, not Works.

We begin where we ended in the previous study, by attempting to answer the question "How can a man be righteous before God?". This chapter is a continuation of a thought that the writer wrote a problem statement for in Romans Chapter 1 and developed a thesis from Chapter 2.

We are cautioned that if Abraham had worked hard to achieve and obtain that which he had, he would have no reason to thank God for it. Instead, Abraham believed God, and it was counted to him for righteousness (v.3). Here we should note that believing is accompanied by obedience, for because Abraham believed, when he was told to move, he did and when he was promised an inheritance, he passed the teaching on to his son. (Deut 29:29).

Verses 4 and 5 answer our question by introducing another facet to it called GRACE. Paul tells us that if you work for something, any reward you get after that is not a gift but payment. Since we established in our previous study that we could never measure up to God's standards, Paul's exhortation here makes total sense: Work not for your righteousness, but believe on Him(Jesus Christ) who justifies the ungodly; then and only then can your faith be counted for righteousness.

Paul also took the opportunity to address an emerging issue that was dividing the church in those days, circumcision. He reminded them that Abraham was counted righteous before the circumcision of the flesh, and it was used only as a seal for the covenant between him and God. (v.9-14) He in this statement directed them that Abraham was the father of both the circumcised and the uncircumcised, by faith. The faith of Abraham is commended in that while he was aware of both he and his wife's natural age he still believed in the son promised to him. (v.17-22)

We are promised that this righteousness can also be imputed upon us if we believe in Him who raised Jesus our Lord from the dead. We are made righteous with Christ! (v.23-25)

I trust we have answered the question sufficiently; we are not made righteous by following a set of rules, or giving alms, or praying and fasting, but by claiming the righteousness of Christ by faith. We do all we do not to be righteous but because WE ARE righteous.

1st Chronicles 4- A Good Father.

This is the genealogy of the sons of Judah the son of Israel. Of all who were named, lived, and died, one man was esteemed above all, whose name was Jabez.

V.3 " ***And Jabez was more honourable than his brethren:"***

This is the report that the Holy Spirit gave of this man of a noble bloodline. We are also taught that he was a praying man, with faith in God of his fathers. One day he;

"called on the God of Israel, saying, Oh that thou wouldest bless me indeed, and enlarge my coast, and that thine hand might be with me, and that thou wouldst keep me from evil, that it may not grieve me!" (v.10)

Jabez prayed for divine blessing, divine expansion/promotion, divine protection, divine provision, and divine deliverance, And because our God is a good Father, He *'granted him that which he requested'*. Our God promises that when we draw near to him He draws near to us. That when we call on Him He will answer us, that when we trust Him He will give us the desires of our hearts.

He promises that when we seek His Kingdom first, everything else, temporal and eternal, shall be added to us. So why not rest easy, like a weaned baby in the arms of our good Father oh wandering soul?

Because the word of God is true and the scripture cannot be broken, the blessing that Israel spoke over the house of Judah in Genesis 49:8-12 is seen here. In verse 38 ' *and the house of their fathers increased greatly'*. v.39-43 is Genesis 49:8 and 11 in action. He fought and defeated his enemy, and dwelt in choice land and peace.

We serve a faithful God, a Good Father.

Psalm 23- The Good Shepherd.

" *The Lord is my shepherd, I shall not want.* "

Can you picture not having a single need or want in your life? Living a life of lacking nothing? I almost cannot, yet the psalmist could proclaim '*The Lord is my shepherd, I shall not want!*' If he had added to the sentence, somehow it would have less meaning than it does, but the Holy Spirit is the author of perfection.

"He maketh me to lie down in green pastures: He leadeth me beside still waters"

Can you picture never lacking spiritual and physical nourishment? Green pastures are the freshest and healthiest for flocks. Still waters are the freshest, the clearest, the coolest, and the safest to drink.

This verse indicates a place of rest. He leads you to places where all your physical, mental, and emotional needs are satisfied; He makes all grace abound toward you so that you can abound in good works. The place of still waters is in Hebrew directly translated as '*He leads me to water in places of repose*', He leads you to drink of the waters of life in the places of rest. In all stages of your spiritual journey, the place the Lord has ordained for you is a place of rest. Want to never come out of rest.

You should be living the reality because our Lord Jesus taught us that we are more valuable than sparrows to the Father. (Matthew 10:29-31, Luke 12:6)

"He restores my soul: He leadeth me in the paths of righteousness for His name's sake."qu

Do you know that thing that runs after sin and is rebellious towards God by nature? Your soul. The Lord works in you both to will and to do His good pleasure. (Philippians 2:13, Hebrews 6:3, 13:20-21). This is the path of righteousness.

The Hebrew transliteration reads '*He renews my life*', the life-giving Spirit of God within you quickens your spirit, soul, and body so that you are never too exhausted or too weak to go on and your health is preserved as you walk with God.

'*He leads me in right paths as befits His name*', the Bible says that the Lord holds His word above all His names, and in this case, this word will be accomplished so that His name and His character could never be held in contempt. As He leads your soul to righteousness, He also leads you in paths where you will achieve and accomplish much so that you will then turn around and say "*Praise the Name of the Lord*'.

"Yea, though I walk through the valley of the shadow of death, I will fear no evil: for thou art with me; thy rod and thy staff they comfort me."

In a more natural sense, for we are in Christ to live in Him and to die is gain (Philippians 1:21). In the spiritual sense, every time we face the enemy in combat we are in the valley of the shadow of death. There is the danger of evil grieving or overcoming us. Hence why we need God with us, because only with Him can we fight and having done, so remain standing. (Ephesians 6:13)

He carries the staff of the Good Shepherd. A staff is used for measuring, for support in walking, as a symbol of office or authority, and when held to look outwards, it can be used as a rod to point a direction or to chasten or correct (Hebrews 12:5-10). When we walk through the valley of darkness, we can trust that our Shepherd is close enough for us to lean on His staff should we feel weak, He will show us the way to walk and when we walk out of the way, His rod will lead us back on to the right path.

"Thou preparest a table before me in the presence of mine enemies: thou anointest my head with oil; my cup runneth over."

In Jewish culture, sitting at the table with someone was an expression of honour, and more so when not servants but the host serves the guests. It was also customary to wash off the heat and dust before sitting at the table, after that, since oil was expensive and precious then, a host offering a guest oil to anoint themselves with was a great honour. Again, the host oiling the head of the guest was the greatest honour. With the food, wine was served, and it was excellent manners to have servants around to refill cups that were running low before the guests could empty them. David bears the testimony here that The Lord Himself prepares and attends to Him at the table, He anticipates His every need! The blessing!

The Lord prepares the table for you not to gloat or grieve your 'haters' or 'doubters' but for His glory. Put on your robes of humility every time the Lord invites you up to the table. With the anointing of the Holy Spirit and the saving blood of Jesus Christ overflowing in your life, what more could you desire? When he thrusts out the enemy for you to destroy, wield the sword in the name of the Lord of hosts. (Deuteronomy 33:27) What comes after a victory is a feast, with The Lord as your host.

"Surely goodness and mercy shall follow me all the days of my life: and I will dwell in the house of the Lord forever. "

'Only goodness and steadfast love will follow me all the days of my life'. Surely means 'it is certain', that goodness and mercy will follow the person described in the preceding verses. Mercy is the love of God that is given to you to cover your faults and shortcomings, goodness is favour, it is God's enabling grace. What Paul expressed in Hebrews 4:16, David had already experienced.

Who among us would not want God's favour and mercy to follow them always? Mercy to cover our faults, and goodness to cover our weaknesses, and in time and eternity to dwell in His presence?

Now boldly declare " The Lord is my shepherd, I shall not want!"

Galatians 3- Children of God by Faith.

I once heard a preacher say that if a sermon does not lead you to remember the cross, then all else is vanity. I venture to suppose that Paul's thoughts were in this line when he called the church in Galatia foolish (v.1) He was rebuking them for how easily they had been swayed by legalism and other doctrines that taught of justification and righteousness wrought by other ways other than the crucifixion of Christ. He was grieved by their turning away from the guidance of the Holy Spirit whom they received when they believed in Jesus Christ. (v.2-5)

He reminded them that salvation is by faith and not by works, (v.6) and "*that they which are of faith, the same are the children of Abraham." (v.7)*

"In thee shall all nations be blessed." (Genesis 12:3) The promise to Abraham was the prophecy of the Messiah, who would not only bring salvation to Israel but to the nations as well. (v.8,9,13,14-18)

Paul also reminded them that reverting to the law of Moses was taking on bondage because righteousness by law is possible only if one keeps every statute of the law. (v.10-12) On the other hand, the just shall live by faith. He also taught and corrected them that Jesus was the fulfillment of the law; for while the law made our transgressions apparent and passed on us the verdict of guilt before our righteous God, the promise of Jesus was given as hope to those who believed. The law was nothing but "*a schoolmaster to bring us unto Christ, that we might be justified by faith."* (v.24) (v.19-25)

The law was fulfilled in Christ for while we were declared guilty of sin before God, Jesus paid the price for our acquittal, that we are now innocent before God through faith in Jesus Christ. (v.26,27)

We as the disciples of Jesus Christ- saved, sanctified, and filled with the Holy Spirit- have put on Christ. Now, *there is neither Jew nor Greek, there is neither bond nor free, there is neither male nor female,* and I would add there is neither black nor white, " *for ye are all one in Christ Jesus.*" (v.28) And if we are Christ's then we are Abraham's seed and heirs according to the promise. Thank you Jesus for what you did on the Cross.

Matthew 9- Pray to be Sent Forth.

Jesus' ministry was marked by teaching, preaching, healing the sick, working miracles, and casting out demons. In this particular chapter, there was a lot of activity in just a day. That is why all of us must strive to mature in the faith, and learn how to exercise the power in us by Christ Jesus. The world needs Jesus, and the only way for them to know and have Jesus is by us Christians not just telling them about Him but living lives that are evidence of Christ's work in us.

"*...And passed over, and came unto His own city.*"v.1

And so it begins... He was greeted by a man on a stretcher sick with palsy. And He, seeing their faith, told him that his sins were forgiven. This is a classic example of standing in the gap; they did for the sick man what he could not do for himself. They brought him to Jesus and believed for his healing and salvation. (v.2-7) I urge you to explore with the Holy Spirit's guidance, the attitude of the scribes in this situation. And because Jesus had already declared that He was here not to seek His glory but that of the Father, so it was(v.8).

"*And passing by He told Matthew "follow me" and he did*" (v.10) without a second thought.

Jesus then sat down to eat with publicans and sinners. Of course, the Pharisees had something to say about it, to which he replied "*... I am not come to call the righteous, but sinners to repentance.*"(v.10-13) He came for you and me!

He then covered the subject of fasting with the disciples of John the Baptist. He acknowledged that fasting was paramount, but said that His disciples would fast after He had been taken away from them. (v14-17)

He also in a parable taught them that His was a new teaching that could not be made to fit into the old or else the vessel/soul would ultimately perish. He was telling them that the keepers of the law of Moses could not also be the bearers of grace. Sometimes the urge in the heart of man is to mix the Gospel and tradition or culture like it is happening in the world right now, or the Word and your forefather's spiritual practices, or the Good News and a few ritual practices once in a while. But for the gospel to be made effective in your life, you cannot pour the new wine of the sacrifice of Christ in the old wineskin. The mindset cannot be ' *I love offering sacrifices to the gods of my ancestors, but they say that Jesus heals and I am sick, so I'll go there for the healing*'. And you cannot put on the righteousness of Christ as a layering piece with what you consider the righteousness you attained of your works in keeping the law.

The word says that our righteousness is as filthy rags before the Lord. Do not do good works to earn righteousness, do good works because you have attained righteousness by grace through faith, which then enables you to perform good works effectively.

While He was speaking, a certain ruler came to beg Him to heal His dead daughter. To think what measure of faith it would take to believe in the dead being made alive again! That's what Jesus did for us by dying on the cross. (v.18,19,23-26) And He as requested " ***but come and lay thy hand upon her, and she shall live.*** " did and she lived.

While He was on the way to the ruler's house, the woman with an issue of blood touched the hem of His garment and by faith, she was healed. (v.20-22) Not just healed, MADE WHOLE.

When He left the ruler's house, "***two blind men followed Him, crying, and saying, Thou son of David, have mercy on us.***" And according to their faith, when Jesus touched them their eyes were opened. (v.27-31)

Immediately they left " *they brought to Him a dumb man possessed with a devil"* (v.32-34) Jesus cast out the demon and the man spoke.

All the occurrences in this chapter made me realise that when Jesus was walking this earth, people who realised who He was and what kind of power He had came to get anything they wanted or needed in their lives. Their background or status did not matter. Much more now that He is glorified and all the power is in His hands, why don't we do that?

While the multitude was marvelled, of course, the Pharisees had something to say. V.35 is a summary of everything Jesus did on this mission.

"But when He saw the multitudes, He was moved with compassion on them, because they fainted, and were scattered abroad, as sheep having no shepherd."

He saw a lot of work that needed to be done, and not enough people dedicated to fulfilling that. But when He ascended, He promised that His disciples would be able to do what He did and more. Indeed there is a lot of teaching, preaching, healing, and working of miracles that need to be done in the world. And the ones to do it are you and I.

What he said next are the most melodious words to the ear:

"The harvest truly is plenteous, but the labourers are few; pray ye therefore to the Lord of the harvest, that He will send forth labourers into His harvest."- (v.35-38)

To think that we all came to the knowledge of the truth because an earthly vessel, like you and I, obedient to the great commission (Matthew 28:18-20) and was willing to be filled by the Holy Spirit and emptied where needed. Now that you have been made a disciple, are you also willing to go out and make disciples of all men? Have you been praying to our Heavenly Father, who is the Lord of the Harvest, to send you out into His harvest, sickle in hand, no conditions, no questions asked? Have you chosen to deny yourself and follow Christ through time and into eternity? Have you been an obedient co-worker? (Luke 9:23, 2nd Corinthians 6:1, 2nd Peter 1:1, 2nd Timothy 2:24, Ephesians 6:6).

My prayer for you is that you will become a worthy labourer for the Father's commissioning, as Christ was, in all faithfulness and humility.

Psalm 15- God cares for your Spirit, Soul, and Body.

3 *rd John 2, 1st Thessalonians 5:23*
We all recognize that our fleshly nature is always contrary to and in constant battle with our spirit (1st Peter 2:11), that is one with the Spirit (John 3:6) To mortify the flesh, many religious institutions and denominations come up with physical rules to counter the works of the flesh, like drinking alcohol is sin and money us evil. Hence some of us we brought up in the faith are sometimes afraid and often ashamed to pray for physical provision, earthly prosperity, and enlightenment of the soul.

On the other extreme is a new crop of 'non-denominational' churches that have no focus on foundational doctrines and teachings (Hebrews 6:1-3), but instead are always harping on about *'financial breakthrough, bigger houses, newer vehicles, manifestation, abundance mindset and giving more if you want to receive more. Their teaching and practice is of excess and lust.'* The focus for them has shifted from who you are because of Christ to what you can get by using Christ's name and they make it seem like material possessions are a measure of someone's faith.

But there is a middle ground, and that is where the grace of God is- God cares about how you dress, eat, and sleep (Luke 12:7, Matthew 6:25,28-34), He is concerned about your mental and intellectual illumination (Psalm 119:130, 113, 66, 49, Proverbs 9:1-6) God cares about your emotional stability and maturity. Just so, He cares about your spiritual growth and eternal salvation. He took on all of you, just as you were and all you had to do was yield. And now in His arms surrender, allow Him to show you His grace and love in every area of your life. Only then can you grow into being:

"He that walketh uprightly, and worketh righteousness, and speaketh the truth in his heart. He that backbiteth not with his tongue, nor doeth evil to his neighbour, nor taketh up a reproach against his neighbour. In whose eyes a vile person is contemned, but he honoureth them that fear the Lord. He that putteth not out his money to usury, nor taketh reward against the innocent. He that doeth those things shall never be moved."- Psalm 15:2-5

This is the person who has discovered the place of rest, he sojourns in the Lord's tent and on His holy mountain. This person can never be shaken…You will not suffer any insecurities, nor seek illicit gain, nor hate anybody in your heart, nor take what does not belong to you, nor beg. The Lord will be your all in all. And you will look forward with the hope of one day dwelling on the Lord's hill for eternity.

Philippians 1- Confidence in God.

It is hard to believe that Paul was imprisoned in Rome when he wrote this letter because it is filled with giddiness and almost childlike excitement. It is the most joyous book in the Bible! Even when Habbakuk wrote that he was rejoicing in the Lord of his salvation, it did not sound this exciting. (Habakkuk 3:17-19)

It speaks of the unique skill that Paul had mastered of looking up to obtain the faith of Jesus Christ and then looking around him with his freshly nourished eyes of faith. We should all learn to look with faith and see God's power and faithfulness made manifest all around us despite our present circumstances and experiences.

Everywhere you see the word 'servant' in the epistles, read it as 'slave', the apostles considered themselves as the lowest form of servant in Christ's work. This speaks to their humility and the revelation of the grace and mercy of God in their lives.

He begins with a benediction as always (v.2-6), praying for them and proclaiming the blessing of God over their lives. He told the church that he was able to pray with joy for them because he was confident that *"He who hath began a good work"* in them *"will perform it until the day of Jesus Christ."* (v.5) God never starts a project He isn't intent on finishing!

Paul also told the church of Philippi that he missed them in Christ (v.7-8), to fellowship together, and edify and encourage one another.

I love the prayer that Paul prays for them: (v.9-11) *'That their love may abound yet more and more in knowledge and all judgement, that they may experience excellence, that they may be pure, sincere and holy until the day of Christ; being filled with the fruits of righteousness (Galatians 5:22-23) which are by Jesus Christ, unto the glory and praise of God.'* He prayed that the love of Christ would help them grow in knowledge and understanding so that it could be in them a measure for all things they hear or experience, and to approve only the excellent things which align with the promises of God in Christ Jesus, and disregard everything else.

And then hc had excellent news for them! (v.12-18) That though he was a prisoner of Rome, it had been to the furtherance of the gospel. Instead of sulking in a corner, he had been preaching the gospel in the palace (Philippians 4:22). And what's more, his being in chains had inspired other Christians in Rome to spread the gospel with much more fervour.

He also said that some were doing it to make fun of him or to gain popularity, you know, ride the Paul fame wave. That was even more good news to him, because **"whether in pretence or in truth, Christ is preached."** Instead of *'exposing false prophets'* and *'correcting corrupt doctrine'* why don't you preach the gospel, dear brethren, only the light can fight the darkness in this world.

Paul urges the church not to be worried about his situation because -he says- it is temporary and it shall turn to his salvation if they instead pray for him, and with their prayer, he was certain that he would eventually be set free. (v.19)

"For to me to live is Christ, and to die is gain."

Paul was not suicidal or depressed, he was declaring a spiritual truth for those who believed. How amazing it would be to go to sleep one day only to wake up to behold the Lord's face (Psalm 17:15). But in the end he says, *'although heaven is beautiful and glorious, you need me here. So I'll stick around so that I can teach you and grow you in the faith some more.'* (v.20-26)

The last few lessons he passes on in the remaining verses are necessary to be learned. (v.27-30)

- *Holiness in conversation-* becoming the gospel of Christ.

- *Unity of the saints in worship and service-* stand fast in one spirit, with one mind (soul) striving together (body) for the faith of the gospel.

- *Courage-* Do not be terrified of your adversaries; spiritual or physical. It is to them evidence of their being children of disobedience but to you of salvation and God.

- *Endurance-* It is given, on behalf of Christ to suffer for His sake.

- *Be encouraged-* Look at what others (Paul) have gone through, endured, and through it attained salvation.

All this begins with us having confidence in God to lead us through it all to him.

When it is dark ahead, He is light upon your path(Psalm 119:105);

When the sea is stormy, He commands the sea to be still (Luke 8:23-25).

When the battle is intense, He will teach you to fight on (Psalm 144:1);

When your resources and capabilities fail you, He will make His grace abound (2nd Corinthians 9:8);

But only if you believe that He is, and He is a rewarder of all who diligently seek Him. (Hebrews 11:6)

Exodus 2- A Compassionate Father.

This chapter is an introduction to the man who was at the core of God's plan to save Israel from slavery in Egypt from before the beginning of time. (Jeremiah 29:11, Genesis 15:13-16) His name was Moses, the son of a man of the house of Levi (v.1), who was later consecrated as priest of the Lord. You all know the story, but I would like to highlight (v.3) how his mother built an ark of bulrushes and pitched it within and without in the manner in which Noah was instructed for his ark. (Genesis 6:14). The pitch is of course a picture of God's grace; it covers our shortcomings within and protects us from external harm. It was a step of faith, and she ended up getting paid to nurse her child.

It is clear that the woman (his mother) brought him up with the knowledge that he was a Hebrew child and when he went back to live in the palace he never forgot. It is what inspired him to defend 'his brethren' against the Egyptians. (11-14) But the time had not yet come for the salvation of Hebrews.

You see, although the 400 years of slavery that the Lord had witnessed to Abraham had elapsed, the children of Israel were still comfortable living in the land of Egypt. They were more satisfied by temporal pleasures than eternal blessings. So what began as a bad act with good intentions earned him rejection from his brethren and hate and murderous threats from Pharaoh, therefore he fled into Midian.

While he dwelt in Midian (v.16-22) God was working on his character to become the meek and humble vessel, the only kind that the Spirit of God can indwell.

Over time, the children of Israel travailed in prayer, seeking God's deliverance, and He looked at them with compassion.

"God heard their cries, and remembered His covenant with Abraham, with Isaac, and with Jacob."

When God looks at you and is filled with compassion toward you, He comes to your aid. Here we also learn the nature and importance of prayer: it is calling on God based on His word, led by His Spirit and it behooved the children of Israel to pray for God to begin moving to their advantage. We pray that His will may be done, according to His covenant with us in His word by His Son.

John 1- The Many Names of Jesus.

As we saw in the previous study, Israel cried out to the Lord, He had mercy on them and sent them the deliverer. Moses is a picture of the Lord Jesus Christ and His mission was a demonstration of the Father's love to us, that while we were yet sinners Christ died for us (Romans 5:8-9). In the same way, while the Israelites while still comfortable in bondage and slavery, Moses gave up his royalty to cling to the promise of deliverance from God.

Let us now explore the many names of Jesus in this chapter. It is by no means an exhaustive list of His many beautiful names, but it is a start:

➤ The Word

"In the beginning was the Word, and the Word was with God and the Word was God. The same was true in the beginning with God. And all things were made by Him; and without Him was not anything made that was." -v.1-3

- Jesus the living Word of God, personified.
- Jesus the Word sent forth in creation.
- Jesus the Creative Word of God.

➤ The Light

" In Him was life; and the life was the Light of men."-v.4

"That was the true Light, which lighteth every man that cometh in the world."- v.9

"He was in the world, and the world was made by Him, and the world knew Him not." -v.10

"But as many as received Him, to them gave He power to become the sons of God, even to them that believe on His name."- v.12

- The light that gave life to our physical births. (Psalm 71:6)

- He made the world, He was the light that was sent into the world in the beginning.

- He is the only source of our salvation, rebirth, and reconciliation to God by grace.

➤ <u>The Only Begotten Son.</u>

"AND THE WORD WAS MADE flesh, and dwelt among us, (and we beheld his glory, the glory as of the only begotten of the Father,) full of grace and truth." -v.14

"No man hath seen God at any time, the only begotten Son, which is in the bosom of the Father, he hath declared him."- v.18

- The one in whom dwells the fullness of God.

- The only one who has seen the face of the Father.

- The one by whom grace and truth came to the world because He is the Word of God.

➤ <u>The Lord.</u>

"He said, "I am the voice of one crying in the wilderness, Make straight the way of the Lord, as said the prophet Esaias." -v.23

- Majestic.
- All power and authority belong to Him.
- He alone is worthy of honour and worship.

➤ <u>The Lamb of God.</u>

"Behold the Lamb of God, which taketh away the sin of the world." -v29b

- The Passover Lamb that was slain for our transgressions.

➤ <u>Son of God.</u>

"Upon whom thou shalt see the Spirit descending, and remaining in him, the same is He which baptizeth with the Holy Ghost. And I swore and bare record that this is the Son of God."- v.33b-34

- The second person of the triune God.
- The one who baptises with the Holy Ghost.
- The only one in whom the Spirit of God abode before Pentecost.
- He is eternal, was before all things, and is after all things.

➤ <u>Master/ Teacher</u>

"Then Jesus turned, and saw them following, and saith unto them, What seek ye? They said unto him, Rabbi, (which is to say, being interpreted, Master,) where dwellest thou?" -v.38

- The one who teaches all Truth.
- All wise and full of knowledge of God.

➤ <u>The Messiah (Christ).</u>

"He first findeth his brother Simon, and saith unto him, We have found the Messias, which is, being interpreted, the Christ." -v.41

● The Saviour of the world.

➤ <u>Jesus of Nazareth, the Son of Joseph.</u>

"Philip findeth Nathanael, and saith unto him, We have found him, of whom Moses in the law, and the prophets, did write, Jesus of Nazareth, the son of Joseph." -v.45

● The son of David by genealogy.
● The Messiah prophesied that He would be born out of Nazareth.

➤ <u>The King of Israel.</u>

"Nathanael answered and saith unto him, Rabbi, thou art the Son of God; thou art the King of Israel." -v.49

● The promised King.

➤ <u>The Son of Man</u>.

"And he saith unto him, Verily, verily, I say unto you, Hereafter ye shall see heaven open, and the angels of God ascending and descending upon the Son of man." -v.49

● The seed of the woman, born of a virgin as the prophets spoke of old.
● The seed promised that would strike the serpent's head.

Deuteronomy 11- Obey and Possess.

Deuteronomy, to me, is a crash course that God offered to Israel on how to survive in the real world after He had been babying them in isolation for almost forty years. If it were an online course today, it would be called " ADULTING 101: How to Behave as You Transition from the Wilderness into the Promised Land." -Do you see it too? Or do I have too much fun with my Bible-

The provision is in the promises, and the fulfillment is in keeping the commandments attached to the promises. These two are the premise for covenant, and our God is a God of covenant. Deuteronomy chapter 11 is just a small portion of how God had designed it so that His people should relate with Him, and through their obedience He could then bless him. God is holy (Leviticus 20:26, 1st Peter 1:15-16).

V1. " *Therefore thou shalt love the Lord thy God, and keep His charge and His statutes, and His judgments, and His commandments always.*"

V.2-7 Moses speaks to the children of Israel and recounts to them how their journey had been from Egypt to where they were then, on the banks of the River Jordan. He in essence told them that God had been faithful to them all those years, so it should be easy for them to keep His statutes and His commandments. He insisted to them that their obedience and faithfulness to God was the only way in which they would be able to be strong and go on to possess their promised inheritance (v.8,9).

"Keep, therefore, all the Instruction that I enjoin upon you today, so that you may have the strength to enter and take possession of the

land that you are about to cross into and possess, and that you may long endure upon the soil that יהוה *swore to your fathers to assign to them and their heirs, a land flowing with milk and honey."*

Let us explore the promised land compared to Egypt:(v.9-12)

EGYPT	CANAAN
Planted seed and had to water it with thy foot. Extremely labour intensive (Genesis 3:17-19)	Flowing with milk and honey. Water from the rain of heaven. The Lord cares for it in all its seasons. (The intention of God to restore humanity to His original plan is expressed here).

Let's also explore the fulfillment that was obedience for the children of Israel and the consequence of disobedience.

Obedience:

★ They would be strong enough to go in and possess the land. (v.8)

★ They would prolong their days in the promised land. (v. 9, 21)

★ The land would receive rain in his due season, the first rain and the latter rain. Whatever is planted grows and they reap plenty of harvest. (v.13,14)

★ There would be grass in their fields for their cattle. (v.15)

★ He would drive out all the nations from before them, and possess greater nations, mightier than themselves. (v. 23)

★ They shall possess everywhere their feet touch. (v.24)

★ No man would be able to stand before them for fear. (v.25)

A blessing for obedience, a curse for disobedience. (v.26)
Disobedience:

Their hearts are deceived and they turn away to serve other gods, these would come upon them (v. 16,17)

- God would be angry with them.

- He would shut up the heavens so that there would be no rain and no harvest. They would perish quickly from the good land that the Lord had given them.

- All they would be able to do to the enemy while walking in obedience, the enemy would be able to do to them if they walked in disobedience.

As we continue to read the rest of the chapter, we learn that the land they were about to possess was naturally a hard land to work, with hills and valleys, hot and dry, and hostile to living things. But the Lord had promised to keep watch over it for their sake, to make sure they prosper in it. Therefore the curse for disobedience is not vindictiveness from God's side, it is because He is just that any of those would befall them. The curse would come not from God punishing them but He just withdrawing His care and protection from them. We are told that God does not tempt man, and neither is He tempted by sin. So as much as He would not try man with sin to see He would fall, in the same way, that if a man falls into sin, the Lord by the nature of Him being Holy could no longer associate with that soul. So the curse befalls the person who is no longer in the Lord's will because they have stopped living under the shadow of the Almighty and are now operating by the natural laws of the fallen world. From Genesis 3 we know that part of it is that the ground would be cursed for man's sake, naturally, it would make yielding its increase to man an extremely strenuous process.

We learn here that obedience and submission to the will of God is a continuous choice, it is not an emotion. It is also not the responsibility of anybody else but you, so choose wisely. Be faithful in your walk as God is faithful and you will begin to experience His promises in your life. One day at a time, on this pleasant walk with Jesus.

No day or time,
Wasted or lost in disuse,
Only peace and plenty will we reap in time,
When our constant companion is Jesus.

Ephesians 2- God Called You Out.

I'm writing to believers, saints, and disciples of our Lord and saviour Jesus Christ; pressing on to receive the prize of the high calling of God in Christ Jesus! But you were not always so...

The old man:

★ Was **dead** in trespasses and sins. (v.1)

★ Walked **according to the course of this world**. (v.2)

★ Walked **according to the prince of the power of the air**. (v.2)

★ Was one among the **company of the children of disobedience**. (v.2,3a)

★ Walked according to the **lusts** of the flesh, fulfilling the **desires of the flesh** and **the mind**. (v.3)

★ By **nature the children of wrath**. (v.3)

★ Was an **alien** from the Commonwealth of Israel. (v.12)

★ A **stranger** from the covenants of promise. (v.12)

★ Had **no hope**, and was **without God** in the world. (v. 12)

You were dead in sin, alienated from God, and therefore could not claim His promises and obtain His provision. You were by nature evil, and loving evil and there was no hope for you in this life or the next. Thank God for His mercy, because like Lazarus from his tomb, Jesus called you out! He made you alive, reconciled you to God, and made you a partaker of all the promises.

And now the new man is:

❖ **Made alive (quickened) by and in Christ.** (v.1, 6a) In this life, our spirits are made alive and in the next life, we have the hope of resurrection.

❖ **Made to sit in the heavenly places in Christ**. (v.6b) We share in Christ's resurrection and ascension. Therefore we can boldly approach the throne of grace(Hebrews 4:16).

❖ **Saved by grace and not works**. (v.8,9)

❖ God's special project in Christ Jesus purposely **to perform good works that God had already planned for us before time began.** You were not an accident looking for somewhere to happen. (v.10)

❖ **Peace has been restored with God**, therefore our spirits are one with the Spirit. (v.13,14, 17) Jesus, by His shed blood, fulfilling the law, broke down the wall that separated man from God.

❖ **Free of the enmity of his flesh to God,** by Jesus the son of God becoming flesh, dwelling among us as a Son of Man, and in His death and bodily resurrection being both Son of God and Son of Man, made us vessels worthy of the Holy Spirit to dwell in. (v.15,16) The new creation by grace is no longer rebellious to God.

❖ <u>**A member of God's household**</u>, no more a stranger or a foreigner, but a citizen. (Galatians 3:26-28) (v.18,19) Through Jesus we have access by one Spirit to the Father.

❖ <u>**A member of the universal church**</u>, the holy temple of the Lord. (v. 21, 22) A habitation of God through the Holy Spirit is being added to daily as more and more people come to Christ.

We are all together being built up as a habitation for God to dwell in in the Spirit.

Genesis 19- You are being Called Forth.

Dear old Lot, although he dwelled among sinful, fleshly, lustful people, yet he was still righteous. He dwelled in a city that was great, and whose dwellers' sin was very grievous. (Genesis 18:20) But while amid all the rot of Sodom and Gomorrah, Lot maintained the right relationship with the God whom he had seen while he dwelled with Abraham. And this is the reason why when he saw the strangers entering the city, he begged them to come and abide with him for the night (Genesis 19:1-4). This is an example of a man who pressed his kindness upon strangers and ended up entertaining angels. (Hebrews 13:1-3)

He beseeched them to go into his house because he knew that the people of the city would seek to do evil upon them if they were to be discovered. I am assuming it was something that occurred regularly because in the evening before they slept the men of the city surrounded Lot's house and demanded *"Bring them out unto us, so that we may know them."* (v.4-8) Here, every kind of sexual perversion is exhibited: rape, homosexuality, sodomy, and fornication. (Deutoronomy 22:5, 2:17-18, Romans 1:25-31) Lot even tried to appease them by offering his daughters to them but they refused. Lot's refusal angered them and where there is strife there is every evil work. (James 3:16) They went on to exhibit pride, anger, violence, wickedness, and vile imagination (Titus 3:3)

"Stand back... This one fellow came in to sojourn, and he will needs be a judge; now will we deal worse with thee than with them." (v.9-10)

The angels of God saved him from mass rape and mob justice among other unimaginable evils. They pulled him back into the house and smote the men outside with blindness. (Luke 4:18, Ephesians 4:18, John 9:25, Isaiah 59:10) (v. 11)

The angels then embarked on the mission they had been sent on by God, and since Jehovah had promised Abraham that the righteous would not perish with the wicked, they had to spirit Lot out of there. His entire household would also be saved by him being found righteous, but some would not listen- ***"But he seemed as one that mocked unto his sons in law"***- Because the gospel of salvation is foolishness to the perishing (1st Corinthians 1:18).

Alas the morning came, and Lot was hesitant, he just would not move. He looked around at his comfortable life, his many cattle and wares, the great city and his family, and his flesh overpowered him. (v.15, 16a)

Thank God for his mercy for he had sent help, the two angels led Lot, his wife, and two daughters out of the city. And when they were outside, one told them ***"Escape for thy life; look not behind thee, neither stay thou in all the plain; escape to the mountain lest thou be consumed." (v.17)***

But Lot was still not ready to give up all of the world's temporal comforts (2nd Corinthians 4:16-18) so he bargained to instead flee to the nearby city. (v.18-21) God granted it to him because His mercy endures forever and He forever holds those He loves.

Lot and his family walked away, but his wife looked back and she was turned into a pillar of salt. (v.26) This is another Eve and the fruit moment, isn't it?

Lot ended up in the mountains after all, but not because of obedience but FEAR (v.30) A double-minded man is truly unstable in all his ways. (James 1:8)

"And God remembered Abraham." -v.29

Dear brothers and sisters, do you heed the call of God every day? Are you walking with Him or are you off in the opposite direction chasing after temporal pleasures? Whatever you do, don't look back! (Luke 9:62) as you'll be unfit for the kingdom of God.

And I leave you with this today: If you let go of God's hand leading you, you will look back, the heart of man is deceitful.

P.S.: There were virgins in Sodom and Gomorrah.

John 12- Dying to Live.

Six days before the Passover feast, five days before the crucifixion, Jesus went back to Bethany *"where Lazarus was which had been dead, whom he raised from the dead." (v.1)*

He went in and together with Lazarus, sat at the table to eat the food being served by Martha. While they were at the table Mary took *"a pound of ointment of spikenard, very costly, and anointed the feet of Jesus, and wiped His feet with her hair: and the house was filled with the odour of ointment." (v.3)* Here we see the demonstration of true worship and service, that spares no cost, esteem or shame. The times when we worship the Lord in truth and spirit, our worship rises to Him as a sweet fragrance, like it filled the room on this day when Mary anointed Jesus' feet. The only other depiction of worship in the Bible that is more glorious than this is in Isaiah 6:1-3, Isaiah's vision of the heaven of God.

We immediately see demonstrated the opposite of that, Judas Iscariot in his pride, selfishness, and jealousy makes a self-righteous statement; *"Why was not this ointment sold for three hundred pence, and given to the poor?" (v.5)* This is exactly what the attitude of Lucifer was before he was thrown out of heaven, as depicted in Ezekiel 28:12-19. The Bible tells us in verse 6 that Judas Iscariot said that not because he cared for the poor but because he was the treasurer and also used to steal from Jesus' ministry funds.

Jesus said *"Let her alone: against the day of my burying hath she kept this. " (v.7)*

The people, when they heard that Jesus was there, flocked to Bethany, to see not only Him but also the man who was raised from the dead. That angered the chief priests and they began plotting to kill Lazarus because his testimony was drawing Jews to follow Jesus! (v.9-11)

The next day, the prophecy was fulfilled (v.12-15) of the King coming riding on a colt. (Zechariah 9:9) Many came from all over, even the Greeks, to see and follow Jesus. And Alas! The hour came (v.23). Many people in the city had come to celebrate Passover, the disciples of Jesus who witnessed Lazarus' resurrection told all about it and many of the strangers turned to follow Jesus. A great multitude welcomed Him into the city, singing and proclaiming. The Pharisees observed 'We *have done nothing to turn people back, they are all following him*', and from then on they began plotting how to kill Him.

Jesus taught something divinely important; that unless wheat falls into the ground and dies it will not bring forth fruit. (v.24)

"He that loveth his life shall lose it, and he that hateth his life in this world shall keep it unto eternal life." (v.25) I call this the principle of multiplication and regeneration. Jesus also demonstrated a core principle of Christianity: submission, by submitting to the will of the Father. Here I would venture to say that without trust, there can never be submission (v.27-28).

"But though he had done so many miracles before them, yet they believed not him.: (v.37)

That the scriptures may be fulfilled. He expressed that the hour of judgement had arrived and the prince of this world would be cast out.

Many, even among the Pharisees believed in Him but hid it because they did not want to be cast out of the temple. Revelation 12:10-11 is a beautiful scripture, especially the last bit " *and they loved not their lives unto death*". In verses 42-43, the chief rulers did, and as such the kingdom of God does not belong. God's commandment is life everlasting. I'll leave you with that for now.

Be encouraged, Jesus died and now lives, that we might have life everlasting. We on our part should die to ourselves every day, so that we may live a life commensurate with holiness. And when the time comes, we should always choose the spear of the enemy rather than bend the knee to the prince of this world. Though we might die in this world, it is so we can live in the next for eternity.

Proverbs 2- The Fear of the Lord

There isn't a direct definition of the fear of the Lord for like holiness, it is a principle that is a principle that doesn't come naturally to man. However, there are words like reverence, awe; attitudes that are a reaction to majesty that come with revelation, associated with the Fear of the Lord. The closest I can come to define the fear of the Lord is by relating it to 1st John 4:18 which says "Perfect love casts out fear". The fear of the Lord is understanding God as love for God is love, and then reacting to His majesty with fear. It is usually expressed through total submission to God. The fear of the Lord is learned, and the Spirit of God is the only teacher (Psalm 24:11-13).

Its first indication is in how we use our tongues. God takes us under His tutelage after we choose to seek to learn the Fear of the Lord (Proverbs 1:7, 3:7-8, Psalm 25:12-ff). The Bible says that fools despise it.

The fear of the Lord is taught only by the Lord, and there are conditions to be met:

❖ Receive the Lord's words and hide His commandments with you (treasure them) v.1 (Isaiah 33:6).

❖ Make your ear attentive to wisdom and incline your heart to understanding (humility and submission, make your mind open to discernment, be open to learning) v.2.

❖ Call out for knowledge/insight and lift up your voice for understanding (prayer) v.3.

❖ Seek her as silver and search for her as for hid treasures (diligent persistent quest for it, seek to find) (psalm 25:14) v.4.

If you do this, then:
"You will understand the fear of the Lord and find the knowledge of God. v.5"
With understanding the fear of the Lord comes a few privileges:

❖ Wisdom from the Lord, knowledge and understanding from His mouth. V.6.

❖ Access to the sound wisdom stored up for the upright by the Lord. Access to the ability to do whatever you put your mind to. v.7(a).

❖ The Lord becomes your shield when you walk in integrity, guarding the paths of justice and watching over your ways. v.7(b), 8.

❖ You gain an understanding of righteousness justice and equity, and every good path. V.9.

❖ Wisdom comes unto your heart, and knowledge will be pleasant to your soul. You will never struggle to learn and always know what to apply when a situation arises. v.10

❖ Discretion/foresight will watch over you, and understanding/discernment will guard you. v.11-19. These together will:

★ Deliver you from the way of evil, from men of perverted speech, who forsake the paths of uprightness to walk in the ways of darkness. Who rejoice in doing evil and delight in the perverseness of evil, men whose paths are crooked, and who are devious in their ways. (could you describe bad company any better?)

★ Deliver you from the forbidden woman, from the adulteress with her smooth words, who forsakes the companion of her youth and forgets the covenant of her God; for her house sinks to Death, and her paths to the departed; none who go to her come back, nor do they regain the paths of life.

The fear of the Lord is our only safety in this world, for the righteous will inhabit the land, (v.20, 21) but the wicked will be cut off from the land, and the treacherous will be rooted out of it, (v.22)

Dear brethren, let us seek to cultivate the fear of the Lord, and then we shall be free from all other fears (Proverbs 14:26).

James 1- God Does Not Tempt Man.

James begins his letter most beautifully- as most apostles did- by introducing himself as a servant (slave) of God and the Lord Jesus Christ (v.1). He is declaring his allegiance and reminding them of their (to be) steadfastness.

"My brethren, count it all joy when you fall into divers temptations;"- v.2

Oh, what a statement, in a world where, then, was full of persecution, vainglory, corrupt doctrine, and all other pressures of life. It is even more precious now; in a world where Christians have begun trying to convince themselves that Christianity should be an easy temptation- free, pressure-free, tribulation-free walk.

He goes on to say

" That the trying of your faith works patience. But let patience have her perfect work, that ye may be perfect and entire (complete), wanting nothing."- v.3-4

The trying of your faith works patience, Galatians 6:9 reminds us not to be weary of doing good. Trying your faith means that there will be instances in your walk when the promises of God on your life will seem too far away and unachievable. Or maybe, it feels like the Lord is taking too long to answer your prayer, do not give up. We have covered the subject of patience in a previous study and concluded that patience is an active verb in a Christian's life. And while you're going through the progression in faith growing into a perfect and complete being, should you face any challenges, worry not.

"If any of you lack wisdom, let him ask of God, that giveth to all men liberally, and upbraideth not; and it shall be given him." (v.5)

And in your temptation, while you are asking God for His help, which He is ever willing to give

"... Ask in faith, nothing wavering. For he that wavereth is like a wave of the sea driven with the wind and tossed. For let not that man think that he shall receive anything of the Lord. A double-minded man is unstable in all his ways." - (v.7-9)

A double-minded man is pulled in two directions simultaneously; he believes God can but is still trying to do by his strength, he prays for God's help and then goes to ask for help from other altars, he trusts God and in the counsel of the world, this man will never prosper in any of his ways.

While we are going through various temptations, one of the virtues we'll cultivate is humility, the realization of our fragility (Psalm 90:12), and helplessness if God is not on our side. Therefore, let he who thinks themselves lowly in life and estate rejoice when he is tempted. Temptation is exaltation, the devil does not fight that which is not important. Likewise, let the rich and highly esteemed rejoice when temptation brings him low because it is a reminder that he like the flower of the grass shall whither and die one day. (v. 9-11)

Let therefore humility grow in us, let us daily humble ourselves before the Lord, that in due season we shall be exalted. (James 4:10-11) We should strive to endure temptation (v.12), for when we overcome, we shall receive the crown of life from the Lord. Let us run the race with endurance, for he is faithful that promised.

For us to endure temptation, we should face it with the right attitude.

"Let no man say when he is tempted, I am tempted of God: for God cannot be tempted with evil, neither tempteth he any man." (v.13)

We should also approach it with the right mind, the old man is constantly striving against the new man. (Ephesians 2)

"Every man is tempted when he is <u>drawn away of his own lust</u> and <u>enticed</u>" (v..14)

Note that temptation has an internal and external element, and the internal is the one that gives power to the external. Once a man is drawn away by his lust, it doesn't matter for what, then the deceiver can send people, personalities, spirits, or create situations for the person to be enticed. We give the devil the power that he uses to steal, kill, and destroy. Whatever is not cast down has to be cast out.

Temptation always begins with the senses and is cultivated in the mind. That is why we should always conform our mind to the mind of God (2nd Corinthians 10:3-6). If not checked, the lust conceives, bringing forth (birthing) sin that is expressed through our members(flesh). When a believer does not feel convicted to repent and turn away from it, and it becomes a habit, it grows into a stronghold.

It is a hard-hearted person that God ultimately gives up to a reprobate mind (Romans 1:27-29). That kind of person continues living in sin, and it is not long before sin is finished with him and brings forth death. (v. 14-15) The Bible says "When sin is finished" because a sinner is a slave to sin (Romans 6:15-16), he does not do it of his free will and it grieves and oppresses him. Thank God for the redemptive blood, and now sin has no dominion over us. This was a warning *"Do not err"*(v.16).

V.17-21 speaks of our conduct as believers and followers of Christ. To put away the sins of the old man, and to put on the garments of righteousness through Christ Jesus.

As we grow in faith, our main weapon to win against temptation is the word of God. Therefore James urges us to be doers and not mere hearers, and that way we shall be blessed in our deeds. (v.22-26) And we are finally warned to not be hypocritical, confessing Jesus with our tongues and speaking out of order with the same, because when we do that our religion is made vain. (v.26)

Finally, *"Pure religion and undefiled before God and the Father is this, To visit the fatherless and widows in their affliction, and to keep himself unspotted from the world."* -v.27

James concludes by saying that true religion is evidenced by love and holiness.

2nd Samuel 8- The Lord our Preservation.

I have discovered that in our spiritual walk, it is not more so much about gaining territory but keeping it. Anybody who has any experience in spiritual warfare knows that if you gain any territory in a battle, if you do not have the skill to hold you will soon lose it; and when/if you do, you will ultimately lose some of what you were previously holding as well. Skill is gained through study and practice and seeking the fear of the Lord. Stamina is gained through exercising your faith for it to grow. (Hebrews 5:12-14) and having a closer walk with God. Sometimes we tend to think that we need God only for the big battles, but the truth is we need God for everything. Small challenges handled poorly usually lead to bigger challenges.

David had a faithful walk with God (1 Sam 13:14; Acts 13:22) and daily pursued after his heart, wisdom, and power. At every turn, he sought God's protection, provision, patience, power, and preservation. Before he did anything, great or small, he sought God first. (1st Samuel 30:8) As it is written in Psalm 51:17 *"The sacrifices of God are a broken spirit; a broken and contrite heart, O God, thou wilt not despise."* God treasures people who are wholly submitted to him.

David's life and exploits are something to admire. He was not perfect, he sinned; but when he sinned he repented and he daily recognised that he needed the Spirit of God (Psalm 51:11-12). The kind of man he was is evident also in how he treated his people and ruled over Israel (2nd Samuel 8:14-15). Under his rule, the nation knew peace and prosperity, and he led all in and to the worship of Yahweh (2nd Samuel 8:11, Galatians 6:14).

In this chapter, we zoom in on seven of David's conquests. He fought and conquered the Philistines (v.1), the Moabites (v.2), Hadadezer the son of Rehob, king of Zobah (v. 3,4), Syrians of Damascus (v.5,6,13) and the Edomites (v.14). In every instance, he fought to win, conquer and subdue the enemy. He was able to maintain and rule over the territory afterward because the Lord gave him victory (v.6, 14) wherever he went.

He gained land, slaves, tributers, much spoil (silver, gold, brass), friends, and new alliances (Proverbs 16:7-31). Toi king of Hamath sent his son Joram to salute him and bless him with many gifts because he had smitten one of his enemies.

We as followers of Christ live in a new dispensation, where our wars are no longer physical as much as they are spiritual; hence our weapons are not spears and arrows. This story is however an important teaching moment on how to conduct ourselves in war, in which we are constantly. Paul in Ephesians 6:10-20 was not writing to the unbeliever but to the believer; when he said to put on your whole armour and fight, but only with the guidance of the Holy Spirit; wait for God to say PURSUE.

Always keep your armour on, and do constant checks to ensure that it is in good condition, stay ready. God bless and keep you, Amen.

Romans 8- There is Therefore Now No Condemnation.

We are not counted righteous because we follow a set of rules or worship on a certain day- we live having been saved from the law of sin unto death- we are counted righteous because we put on the righteousness of Christ. Having been saved by grace through faith,

"There is therefore now no condemnation to them which are in Christ Jesus, who walk not after the flesh, but after the Spirit."-v.1

We walk after " the law of the spirit in Christ Jesus" which has freed us from the law of sin and death (v.2) (Romans 7:12-25). And in us, the righteousness of the law is fulfilled, since Jesus took on and died with our sinful nature. (v.3,4)

Thank God that we are redeemed, because "to be carnally minded is death." (v.6,7) We as humans, without the nature and power of Christ are vile and unholy before God and are His enemies. (v. 8) The single most important mark of a disciple of Christ is having the Spirit of Christ (v.9-10). And the Spirit makes us alive because of righteousness. And the most beautiful aspect of it is it makes us dead to sin! We are not tempted by it, not ruled by it, not grieved by it, or even condemned by it. What's more, we have the promise of resurrection of the body unto eternity. (v.11,13)

Are you a son/daughter of God? If you're continuously and constantly led by the Spirit of God then you are! (v.14) You are free from bondage to fear, and have been adopted into the beloved, and can boldly cry "Abba Father" (v.15,16)

"And if children, then heirs, heirs of God, and joint heirs with Christ."-v.17

Having this blessed assurance, we can then rejoice in our sufferings and tribulations, because if we can suffer with Christ then we will be glorified and exalted with Him at the close of this age. (v.17, 18)

The writer of Romans also teaches us a beautiful fact: that all creation suffered when man fell from glory in the garden of Eden, hence they are all awaiting the day they will be set free from the bondage of corruption. The whole creation is praying and hoping for Christ's second coming, and when He appears we too shall appear with Him. (Colossians 3:4)They are looking forward to Christ's righteous rule (New Jerusalem) (v.19-23). We await the day when death shall be defeated, and we shall be freed from corruption and decay.

In the present world, creation is looking forward to every time one of the sons of God by faith in Christ matures and begins to exercise dominion and rule over them. We who are indwelled by the Holy Spirit have the quickening power of God in us, therefore anything we do, touch, or influence also receives that same life. This is the life that gives all creation that we interact with relief and salvation from the pain of corruption and decay. As we saw in Deuteronomy 11, God watching over land means that it no longer has to struggle to bear, and since we carry the presence of God, we are tools to be so used in His service.

Let us therefore be patient in that hope (v.24,25) And in the days when our strength fails us, our knowledge falls short, the spirit Himself prays for us before God with groanings which cannot be uttered (v.26, 27) according to the will of God.

Hold on to faith; for all things work together for good because you love God and are called according to His purpose (v.28). His purpose is laid out as follows: based on His *foreknowledge*, He *predestinated* you to be conformed to the image of His Son. Based on His predestination outside of time, in time He *called you* then, *justified* (v.33) you, and *glorified you.* Justified means that before God you are just as if you've never sinned and glorified means that you are enthroned and exalted with Christ.

Having learned about His great eternal purpose, we can rightly and with conviction answer this question:

"He that spared not His own Son, but delivered Him up for us all, how shall He not with Him also freely give us all things?"- v.32

Jesus Christ who died for our justification also daily intercedes for us in God's throne room. (v.34) Since He who loved us sent His Son to die for us (John 3:16), now that He has made us alive in Him, nothing can separate us from the love of God in Christ Jesus (v.35-36). When facing tribulation, distress, persecution, famine nakedness, peril, or sword, we are more than conquerors through Him that loved us. (v.37)

When facing death or life, angels or principalities, or powers, or things present, or things to come, or height, or depth, or any other creature, we shall remain safe and secure in the Love of god in Christ Jesus our Lord. (v.38,39)

Isaiah 53- Christ made Intercession for Sinners

One day, not so long ago, I asked the Lord a question, "If we are living under the New Covenant, what is the point of learning about the old? Why is the Old Testament written out in such detail?" This question prompted God, in His grace, to open a new dimension of revelation that I am still (thankfully and humbly) exploring. You see, I had gotten to a point where the Bible was beginning to be too ordinary and too familiar to me. The Old Testament more so, sounded like a collection of old stories that I knew but could not rightly relate to. It is that question that birthed this devotional series!

The part of the answer that I have learned so far is that all scripture when the Holy Spirit teaches it to you points you back to Jesus Christ, (John 16:13-15) our Lord, the Lamb of God slain for the atonement of our sins. Isaiah 53 does this by giving us a picture of Christ's death on the cross.

In the Old Testament, the atoning sacrifice was offered to die in place of the souls of the children of Israel (Leviticus 4-7, Exodus 29-32). The atoning sacrifice was supposed to be healthy and without blemish and in the silver offering, both the rich and the poor were required to offer the same amount; because one soul is as valuable as the next in God's eyes.

The writers of the Gospel are very economical with the details of Jesus' death on the cross, perhaps the Holy Spirit knew He had already covered all the bases in the Old Testament. (John 19:19-42)

Let us explore Isaiah 53.

Jesus:

- Would be of ordinary ancestral descent (John 1:46).

- Would be despised and rejected by men, who would subject Him to suffering (Matthew 27:20,26, Luke 23:22-25).

- Would experience sorrow and grief (Matthew 27:46).

- Bore our griefs and our sorrows (v.4).

- Was wounded for our transgression, bruised for our iniquities, with His stripes we received healing (v.5).

- Would be the lamb that was offered as the atoning sacrifice for us all. (v.6, Luke 23:48).

- Would bear the punishment and affliction, He was scourged and derided, yet He never opened His mouth (v.7).

- Would be put to death despite Him being innocent (Luke 23:22).

- Would make His grave with the wicked, and in His death with the rich (Luke 23:33, 50-53).

- Had done no violence, neither would any deceit be found in his tongue (v.9, James 3:2).

- Yet it would please the Lord to bruise Him so that His soul would be a sin offering for us all (v.10, Luke 23:24, Matthew 27:46, Galatians 1:4).

• Would pour out His soul unto death, bearing the sin of many, and making intercession for the transgressions.

• It would please the Father to exalt Him. (v.12, Ephesians 1:7, Colossians 1:113-22).

Jesus on the cross:
Was punished that we might be forgiven,
Was made shame that we might receive His glory,
Was rejected that we might be accepted.
Died our death that we might enjoy His life,
Was hated of God that through Him love may be fulfilled,
Bore our weakness, so that we might gain His strength.
He rightly said, "It is finished!".

> *"But GOD chose to crush him by disease,*
> *That, if he made himself an offering for guilt,*
> *He might see offspring and have long life,*
> *And that through him GOD's purpose might prosper.*
> *Out of his anguish, he shall see it;*
> *He shall enjoy it to the full through his devotion.*
> *"My righteous servant makes the many righteous,*
> *It is their punishment that he bears;*
> *Assuredly, I will give him the many as his portion,*
> *He shall receive the multitude as his spoil.*
> *For he exposed himself to death*
> *And was numbered among the sinners,*
> *Whereas he bore the guilt of the many*
> *And made intercession for sinners." -v.10-12*

Blessed be the name of the Lord and Saviour Jesus Christ now and forever.

Mark 15- It Is Finished.

(Read also Luke 23, Matthew 27, John 18, 19)

(R)Before we begin today's exposition, I should highlight this: you know the popular image (made by man) of Jesus on the cross with the hands and feet nailed and His side pierced, and a little aesthetically pleasing blood flowing out. A nicely adjusted crown of thorns on his head, a handsome unphased face, and a tastefully wrapped swaddling clothe on His crotch? It is not a real depiction of affairs.

Jesus hung on the cross naked, His skin ripped apart from scourging in the hands of the chief priest and the Roman soldiers. His bones we not broken so He bled all the life out of His flesh, they stripped His clothes and cast lots for them. He had not eaten or drunk anything for a day and a night so His lips were probably cracked and chapped. He was being mocked and reviled so His countenance was mired with shame and grief, He was dehydrated at His death so chances are you could count His ribs quite easily. He hung there for six straight hours so He was sunburned and His skin had quite probably begun to hang on to His bones. He died an ashamed, rejected, reviled, and hated man, and thank God He did because there is no greater sacrifice.

With this in mind, let's now walk through the chapter:

- He was falsely accused and He did not defend Himself (v.1-5).
- He was delivered to die for envy (v.9-11).
- He was condemned to be crucified by His people (v.12-14).

- He was scourged, and beaten with a stripping leather thong (v.15).
- He was mocked and a crown of thorns was placed on His head (v.17-20).
- He was physically weakened (v.21).
- He was given vinegar to drink (v.23).
- He bore accusations (v. 26).
- He was crucified among thieves (v. 28).
- He was rejected and hated by His people (v.29).
- He was forsaken by the father unto death. (v.34).
- He suffered unto death (v.37).

The priests instructed the people to shout '*Crucify Him!*' and even went as far as to accept the guilt of His innocent death. Pilate knew that He was delivered because of envy, we have highlighted it in previous studies. He surrendered Him to them to do with as they pleased. They stripped Him, mocked, flogged, and debased Him and after that they crucified Him. The accusation of His cross was "*King of the Jews*".

And because of what He endured we:

❖ We were reconciled back to God (v.38).

❖ The faith and gospel were made available even to the Gentiles (v.39).

❖ There was presented an opportunity for Joseph of Arimathea to proclaim his faith (v.43-46) and we have the same privilege today.

Thank you Jesus for your sacrifice on the cross, you gave all so that we can have all things. Thank you for the gift of salvation.

Psalm 22- Calling on The Father.

It seems that the Holy Spirit still has much to teach us about the crucifixion, the cross, and the value of Christ's sacrifice on that day.

Psalm 22 is among the most beautiful of David's songs. It is the Spirit of God speaking through the mouth of David about Christ's experience and thoughts from the night before His crucifixion to when He ascended from the dead, and why He endured it all. If you are ready, let's look up at the cross and with reverence climb up onto it beside Him, and begin to look down, around, and within Him.

Down and Around...

- *But I am a worm, and no man: a reproach of men, and despised of the people.* (v.6, Isaiah 53:3)

- *All they that see me laugh me to scorn... they shake the head saying, He trusted in the Lord that He would deliver Him...*

(v.7,8, Matthew 27:39-43).

- *Be not far from me; for trouble is near; for there is none to help.* (v.11, Luke 23:46)

- *For dogs have compassed me: the assembly of the wicked have inclosed me: they pierced my hands and my feet* (v.16, 17, Matthew 27:22).

- *They put my garments among them and cast lots upon my vesture* (v.18, John 19:23-24).

Within...
SON OF MAN.

- *My God, My God, why hast thou forsaken me?* (v.1-5, Matthew 27:46). Pain, suffering, rejection, and hope of salvation are expressed here.

- *But thou art He that took me out of the womb:... thou art my God from my mother's belly.* (v.9-10). Reverence, worship, obedience, trust; allegiance to the Most High God.

- *But be not thou far from me, O Lord: O my strength... Deliver my soul from the sword.* (v.19-21) Helplessness and weakness submitted to the all-powerful God.

- *I will declare thy name unto my brethren: amid the congregation will I praise thee.* (v.22-23) Praise and thanksgiving to Yahweh, the purpose for Christ to die was so that God would be preached to the whole world. (1st Thessalonians 5:18)

SON OF GOD.

- *...neither hath He hid His face from Him; but when He cried unto Him He heard (v.24)-* That God sent His son was an answer to the cry of His people.

- *... I will pay my vows before them that fear Him (v.25).* Jesus was willing to die for the people's salvation.

- *The meek shall eat and be satisfied... your heart shall live forever (v.26)*. Jesus is the bread of life, the source of everlasting life.

- *All the ends of the world shall remember and turn unto the Lord... For the Kingdom is the Lord's (v.27-28)*- God's plan to reconcile the whole Adamic race back to Him through the sacrifice of Jesus Christ.

- *All they that be fat upon the earth shall eat and worship: all they that go down to the dust shall bow before Him: and none can keep alive His own soul (v.29)* God is the giver of all life and will make those who died in Him to live again. Christ kept His soul alive!

- *They shall come, and shall declare His righteousness unto a people that shall be born, that HE HATH DONE THIS* (v.30-31)- CHRIST'S ESTABLISHED KINGDOM IS AN EVERLASTING KINGDOM.

Brethren, Jesus' death on the cross was the ransom for all the souls on all the earth, and all the times. I urge you therefore to receive the new life with gratitude and work out your salvation as the Spirit enables you.

Matthew 4- Let Me Tell You About Jesus.

Today, I would like to tell you about Jesus, the man He was while He walked the earth. Our story begins with Him being *"led up of the Spirit into the wilderness to be tempted by the devil" (v.1).*

Jesus fasted for forty days to empty Himself before God. We saw it with Moses as well, when He went up Mount Horeb (Exodus 34:28-35) to receive the commandments. He had to humble and afflict his fleshly nature before the Spirit and power of God could operate through him.

After those forty days, Jesus was hungry (v.2). The tempter saw an opportunity and he approached.

The first temptation:

"If thou be the son of God, command that these stones be made bread."-v.3

Satan was trying to appeal to the prideful nature of man in this instance by questioning Jesus' confession and hence the integrity and character. He was also trying to appeal to the lust of the flesh, by tempting Him to tend to a natural appetite. But Jesus said:

"It is written, man shall not live by bread alone, but by every word that proceedeth out of the mouth of God."- v.4, John 4:34

The second temptation:

"The devil taketh Him up unto the HOLY CITY, and setteth Him up on a PINNACLE OF THE TEMPLE. And saith unto Him, if thou be the Son of God, cast thyself down: for it is written, He shall give His angels charge concerning thee..."- v.5-6

The devil then attempted it a second time, by taking Jesus to the highest city in Israel, the city on a hill, and placing Him on the highest point of the city. From there, the fall would be steep. And from there looking down, satan questioned the validity and truthfulness of God's word. As he did in the garden of Eden, he questioned the character of Yahweh (Psalm 91, Genesis 3:4-5). Again, Jesus knowing and trusting God answered:

"<u>It is written again</u>, thou shall not tempt the Lord thy God." -v.7

At that moment, satan had forgotten that as much as he had rebelled he was still God's creation, when Jesus said to him *"Thou shall not..."* was in a way a humiliating moment for him. Should Jesus have seen the need to jump, he possibly would have been instructed to catch Him. God IS, and Jesus knew that to put the character of God to the test is a sin. And He in a way taught us how to deal with doubt either from within or without, swing the sword of the Spirit at it, you will never miss.

The third temptation:

"Again, the devil taketh Him up onto an exceeding high mountain, and sheweth Him all the kingdoms of the world, AND THE GLORY OF THEM: and saith unto Him, all these things will I give thee, if thou will fall down and worship me."- v.8,9

Subtle satan, trying to provoke the lust of the eyes with the glory and the kingdoms of the world. What Satan has always done -what he offered to Adam and Eve- was autonomy from God, independence from God. But Jesus knew that it was hell HE was actually being offered.

"Then saith Jesus unto him, Get thee hence satan; for it is written, Thou shalt worship the Lord thy God, and Him only shalt thou serve."-v.10

He had passed the test, the devil left him and the angels came and ministered to Him.

Jesus was tempted, and received victory, He won. With victory came the power of the Holy Spirit, what He needed to minister here on earth.

Jesus then began His ministry:

- He taught repentance, to prepare for the kingdom of God (v.17).

- He recruited the disciples (v.19-21).

- He taught in the synagogues and preached the gospel of the kingdom (v.23).

- He healed all manner of diseases (v.23).

- He delivered those possessed and oppressed by demons (v.24).

- He delivered the mentally challenged (v.25).

By resisting the tempter in the wilderness, He gained the power to overcome the enemy and the oppressor and to teach with conviction because the Word of God had become experiential for Him: He not only knew and believed, but He had also tested and seen that the Lord is good (Psalm 34:8-9).

2nd Chronicles 29- Repent.

Let's talk about Hezekiah, king of Jerusalem. I should begin by saying that God does not override the will of human beings, so it is always upon us to choose God. If we draw near to Him, He draws near to us (Psalm 73:28, Hebrews 10:22,23) and vice versa.

There are several successive steps that King Hezekiah led the congregation of Israel through to be restored to the Lord God:

> <u>Repentance.</u>

First, we are told that he did what was right in the sight of the Lord, just as his father David did (v.2). Repentance was necessary because the people had sinned in turning away from following the Lord. Repentance means to turn away from and renounce your old ways, and turning to do that which is good in God's sight.

- He opened the doors of the house of the Lord and repaired them (v.3).

- He brought back the Levitical order and commanded them to sanctify themselves and the house of the Lord, and "carry forth the filthiness out of the holy place". (v.4,5)

- Repented for the sins of their forefathers and the rebellion of their ancestors (v.6,11).

Note here that repentance is a change of heart that is then expressed as a decision and an action. It is a process, although short.

➤ <u>Sanctification.</u>

As the people had admitted that they had done that which was evil in the sight of God, they then began to walk back to Him. This is achieved through sanctification, for God is holy, He can't interact with the unholy or dwell in an unholy place.

- The Levites sanctified themselves (v.12-15).

- They cleansed the temple, the house of the Lord (v.15).

- They brought out all the uncleanness that they found in the temple of the Lord and threw it out. (v.16-19)

- They then presented the sanctified items to the Lord.

➤ <u>Sacrifice.</u>

"Then Hezekiah the king rose early, and gathered the rulers of the city, and went up to the House of the Lord."- v20.

- They brought animals for the sin offering (v.21,22).

- They made a propitiation/ atonement offering for their sins (v.23).

- They offered the sacrifice of thanksgiving and praise (v.25-27, 30).

- They offered the sacrifice of worship and service before the Lord (v.28, 29).

After all these, the Lord drew near to them, and the reconciliation began.

➤ <u>Restoration.</u>

Their fellowship with Yahweh was restored and the congregation brought willingly to the house of the Lord gifts, material goods, their hearts, and minds. (v.31-33)

➤ <u>Justification.</u>

They came unto God of a clean heart, and He justified them. (v.31) He absolved them of all the guilt and consequences of sin.

➤ <u>Revival and Renewal.</u>

This is always God-ordained. When the Lord touched their hearts, they gave until the Levites alone could not handle the service of the Lord.

Everything was set in order, the Lord's dwelling was restored, hence the Lord could be their God and dwell amongst them once more.

And they all rejoiced and thanked God, *"that God had prepared the people: for the thing was done suddenly. " (v.36)*

Repentance is the only way we can begin to walk back to the way (of) Christ.

Luke 18- Pray and Faint Not.

J esus taught in parables often and on this day He taught
"That man ought to always pray, and not to faint." -v.1
He taught what manner of prayer we ought to sustain: patient, in humility, driven by faith, sacrificial, believing in God's all-powerful nature, and the name of Jesus. Let's explore each, by looking at the demonstrative parable:

Patience.

He began by telling them about a judge in a city who did not fear God nor had any respect for any man. A widow came to him seeking justice but he would not grant it. The widow kept going back and she eventually wore him down. He granted her request only because she could not give up. v.2-8 Jesus told this to demonstrate that God will always avenge His elect who pray and cry to Him day and night though sometimes it feels like it is taking too long if they keep the faith (Revelation 2:3, James 5:11, James 1:3, Hebrews 12:11). For if we hope for that which we do not see we do so with patience (Romans 8:25).

Humility.

Jesus told the next parable to warn against self-righteousness and pride by laying out the prayers of two men: a pharisee and a publican.

The Pharisee went before God singing his accolades, saying that he was not like other men who were extortioners, unjust, adulterers, or even as the publican praying beside him (v.10-12).

The publican walked to the back of the temple and would not even lift his eyes unto heaven (attitude of worship and reverence) and all he could manage was *"God be merciful to me a sinner." (v.13)*

Jesus emphasised that the publican went to his house more justified than the former,

"for everyone that exalteth himself shall be abased, and he that humbleth himself shall be exalted."- v.14

(Matthew 18:4, Philippians 2:8, Colossians 3:12, James 4:6-10, 1st Peter 5:6)

Faith.

Little children were brought to Him to be blessed, but the disciples wanted to forbid it. He corrected them and even taught them that only those who receive the Kingdom of God as a child should inherit it (v.16-17). The attitude of a child is trusting, not marred with unbelief, and daily believing that He who promised will also do it (Matthew 6:30, 16:18, Romans 10:17, Isaiah 28:9, Psalm 131:2).

Sacrificial.

Prayer is communion with God, therefore we should go to Him with the attitude of sacrificing our wills, desires, and ambitions, laying them all aside so that His will and purpose may prevail. You could keep all the laws and commandments, but if you are doing it to earn your righteousness it is all for nothing. (v.18-25) The ruler had kept all the laws of Moses since his youth, but when Jesus told him to sell all and distribute to the poor he could not do it. He esteemed his riches higher than a relationship with God (Luke 9:62, Mark 4:19, Romans 13:14, Galatians 5:17). We should daily depend on the grace of God for the flesh wars against the spirit.

Believing in the Omnipotence of God.

When Jesus had demonstrated to the disciples that nobody would be justified in his righteousness, he was asked *"Who can be saved?" (v.26, 27)* to which he answered, *"The things which are impossible with man are possible with God."*

We have to pray and live believing in the all-powerful God, if we are like Abraham in Genesis 20:11, we might end up living a life stained with willful sin.

In the name of Jesus.

Finally, the blind man called on the name of Jesus of Nazareth, and when he believed he received his sight. (v.37-43) We should always pray in the name of Jesus, the name above all names. (2nd Timothy 2:19, Hebrews 1:4, 13:5, colossians 3:17, Philippians 2:8-11).

As we call on the name of Jesus, let us all purpose to also cultivate the traits of Jesus in ourselves and others.

Numbers 12- The Way Up is Down.

Picture the children of Israel in the wilderness, camped around the tent of the Tabernacle. To the east, west, north, and south, they had set camp as directed by Jehovah. It was a rest day from the journey so everybody had a little bit of free time on their hands.

While everybody else was tending to whatever or whoever needed tending to, Miriam and Aaron utilised their time to speak against Moses because he had married an Ethiopian woman (v.1). According to them, he was not fit for any kind of relationship with the Lord. (v.2)

The Bible tells us why the Lord had decided it so because;

"Moses was very meek, above all the men which were upon the face of the earth." - v.3

God would have none of that, he corrected Miriam and Aaron's bad attitude immediately. He explained to them that apart from being humble, Moses was also faithful (v.7, 8) and ventured to ask them why they were so apt to condemn the Lord's anointed. They did not answer.

The Lord was angry with them, and he punished Miriam by inflicting her with leprosy for a week (v.10-16).

It is interesting that when Miriam became leprous, Aaron turned to plead with Moses instead of God, why do you think that was?

"And Aaron said to Moses, "O my lord, account not to us the sin which we committed in our folly."- v.11

Moses pleaded with the Lord to forgive them. *"So Moses cried out to יהוה, saying, "O God, pray to heal her!" -v.13* The Lord however made it clear that she needed the lesson, therefore she was shut out of the camp for seven days.

The Lord requires a humble spirit and a faithful heart before He can deal with us, not just as children but as mature heirs together with Christ.

Think to yourself, you may get to heaven, but what report will you have to present to our Judge and King? Of good or dead works? Of faithfulness or slackness? Of obedience or rebellion?

Only two people in the Bible stated that they kept the faith to the end, Paul and Jesus, and the one trait they had in common was meekness/ humility.

The way up is down.

Colossians 2- New Age, Same Old Deception.

(E zekiel 11:19, 18:4, 20, 30, 32.
Ezekiel 31:10- pride self-worship
Ezekiel 33:13- the whole law/need for Christ's righteousness.)

Paul had diagnosed the condition of ailing the church in Colossae, and it is a condition that is currently ailing the church. Impatience, worry, immaturity, and lack of acknowledgment of the true head of the church. (All these are expressible symptoms but...) he was warning them against being turned away from the cross of Christ by some vain/false teachings that sounded good to the ear and appeased the senses.

He prayed for them " ***that their hearts might be comforted, being knit together in love, and unto all riches of the full assurance of understanding, to the acknowledgment of the mystery of God, and of the Father, and of Christ; in whom are hid all the treasures of the wisdom of God.***"- v.2,3

He prescribed the treatment for the condition as looking up to God and surrendering to Him in whom are hid all the treasures of the wisdom of God. Notice that he said "HID", meaning you have to seek it; it is acquired by a diligent, enduring, patient seeking of the face of God. (Proverbs 25:2, 2:4, 8:17). The wisdom of man on the other hand is readily available to those who will not seek the wisdom of God. (v.4)

The knowledge and wisdom of man or any other source, whose seeds are plants through beguiling ***"with enticing words."*** (v.4), are:

★ Philosophical teachings (Socrates, Plato, etc.) (v.8)

★ Vain deceit (teachings that seek to exalt the self).

★ Traditions of men (Jesus and culture verse) Rudiments of the world (enneagrams, agnosticism, pantheism, universalism).

★ Deceive you from gaining your reward in voluntary humility (Buddhism, Yoga). (v.18). Worshipping of angels (spirit guides, channelling, worshipping of gods and goddesses) Intruding into things he has not seen.

★ Vainly puffed up by the fleshly mind (manifesting, positivity, meditation).

★ Not holding the Head who is Christ (v.19) The teachings offered do not lead back to Christ and His love and sacrifice for us.

★ Subject to ordinances after the commandments and doctrines of men (religious slavery, the Book of Mormonism, Jehovah's Witness).

★ A show of wisdom in will worship, and humility, and neglecting of the body; not in any honour to the satisfying of the flesh (v.23) some form of godliness.

★ Judging in meat, drink, or respect of a holy day, or the new moon, or the sabbath days (v.16) Legalism.

The only way to resist false teaching is by submitting to God, resisting the devil and he will flee. We should also seek to be taught the wisdom and knowledge of God by the Holy Spirit. In God are hidden all the treasures of wisdom and knowledge, and by daily taking up our cross and following Christ, it is revealed to us as the Word of God.

❖ As we received Christ, so we should walk in Him (v.6), and we received Him in faith.

❖ Rooted and built up in Him, established in the faith, abounding in thanksgiving (v7), which is a testimony of our hope in Him.

❖ We should walk in the full assurance that in Christ dwells all the fulness of the Godhead bodily (v.9), we glory in His resurrection and glorification.

❖ We are complete in Him, who is the head of all principality and powers (v.10) therefore we need not fear Satan, his angels or demons, and other workers of iniquity.

❖ We put off the body of the sins of the flesh. (v.12,13) and made alive unto righteousness.

❖ We were buried with Him in baptism and raised with Him through the operation of God (v.12).

❖ We are forgiven all our trespasses (v.13).

❖ Blotting out all ordinances against us (v.14, 15), nailing them to the cross. There is therefore no condemnation against us.

❖ He triumphed against the enemy, therefore we are made more than conquerors.

Deuteronomy 20- Who Can Stand against the Lord?

The Lord through Moses continued to give the children of Israel instruction on how to conduct themselves when they came into their land of inheritance. In this chapter, the emphasis was on their conduct during times of war.

"When thou goest out to battle against thine enemies, and seest horses, and chariots, and a people more than thou, be not afraid of them: for the Lord thy God is with thee, which brought thee out of the land of Egypt." -v.1

It is important to have an occurrence to reference when you are facing a challenging situation. Trials and testations are meant to perfect our faith, in this case, the children of Israel had their salvation from bondage in Egypt; *'If He did that, He will do this too.'*

The first thing He told them was to never be afraid of the enemies' armies every time they went into battle, that a priest should remind people *"Fear not, and do not tremble, neither be ye terrified because of them. "* *(v.2-4).* Because the Lord God promised He would be the one to go with them and fight with them. (perfect love casts out fear), He also insisted on the importance of steadfastness (Luke 9:23)(v.5-8). He told them that anybody who had anything to make them double-minded or distracted at war should be allowed to turn back from marching towards the enemy. Only those who were dedicated should be allowed in the army.

The Lord also insisted on the importance of each soul to Him, by commanding that Israel should always declare peace first. (v.10-12) If they surrender, then they wouldn't have to die.

The Lord told them that if a city should want to make war then they should besiege it because He would deliver it into their hands. (v.13-15) And take the spoils of the war and make tributaries of their women and children. But this was only for the cities which were outside the boundaries of their inheritance.

Of the nations which occupied the land the Lord had given to them for an inheritance, no soul would be left alive (v.16). All the nations; the Hittites, the Amorites, the Canaanites, the Perizzites, the Hivites, and the Jebusites were to be annihilated. (v.17) This was to avoid spiritual and moral corruption (1st Corinthians 15:33)

"That they teach you not to do after all their abominations, which they have done unto their gods; so should ye sin against the Lord your God." (v.18)

Finally, they were told not to cut down trees unnecessarily, seeing as God had created them for their increase (v.19-20, Genesis 1:29-30) and also to feed animals.

The lessons I have learned from this study are:

- You should not fear the enemy when God is in battle.

- Anything that is not cast down has to be cast out. You have to guard against all possible sources of corruption.

- God is in charge of everything.

Mark 3- Kingdom Against Kingdom.

This chapter serves to make it clear that there is no neutrality in spiritual matters, there are two sides and you must pick one. The raging battle is between the kingdom of God and the kingdom of Satan. It is why Paul urged us in Ephesians to put on the whole armour of God, so that when we face the adversary we all look the same, like Jesus.

Some ways that the devil fights the children are highlighted here: legalism, materialism, evil thoughts, anger, grieving the Holy Spirit, and insighting division in the body of Christ.

Legalism is man adding to the laws of God and trying to earn righteousness by keeping them. In this instance, it had become customary that on the Sabbath one could not offer medical assistance unless it was a life-and-death issue. In churches today, such laws as not wearing makeup, dancing in the church, and who to associate with are imposed as a standard of holiness.

Jesus made it clear that the Sabbath was a gift to man from God as a day of rest, not of taking on more burdens. He also healed a man with a withered hand to deal with the malady of legalism in their hearts (v.1-6).

Another observation here is that people followed Christ for what they could get from Him, not for who He was (v. 10,11). The thoughts of the multitude were leaning towards the material world more than eternity, they were more interested in saving their bodies than their souls.

V.12 is a foreshadowing of how the war of kingdom against kingdom will end, with Christ as the victor.

We also see that each kingdom needs willing workers and soldiers. The battle is spiritual but the battleground is here on earth, so the children of man must get involved. Jesus called to Himself those whom He willed and by their free will chose to follow Him (v.14-19). Our response to the calling will determine which side of the battle we will end up on. God made the twelve disciples one unit in Christ, to work towards the same goal and by the same power. He also called them to *"Be with Him"*, become a part of Him, and become one body, like we are the communion of saints.

At one time, evil thoughts consumed the religious leaders and they accused Jesus of being in league with the prince of the demons and using his power to cast out evil spirits. He countered them with an illustration saying that a kingdom divided against itself shall not stand. And because they all knew Satan's kingdom was not divided, He then introduced to them the fact of power. Only one stronger than the strongman could bind up the strong man (v.22-25). Jesus was teaching them that He was from the kingdom of God, which was mightier than the kingdom of Satan. Satan's works are lying signs and wonders.

The church (invisible body) is made up of those whom God has called by the Holy Spirit and brought unto Himself. That is why Jesus said that His followers were His brothers and sisters. In v. 20, His family came by to try and take Him away because to them He was *"out of His mind"*, but it was because they were not joined to Him and therefore had no revelation of His true nature and mission. Those who did are whom He called His family (v. 31-35).

He also taught of the unforgivable sin of blaspheming the Holy Spirit, the unforgivable sin is a verbal sin. The Bible says that out of the fullness of the heart the mouth speaks, so what a person speaks he also believes. So the Pharisees believed that Jesus was operating by the power of an evil spirit and they accused Him of it. In calling the Holy

Spirit evil, they had blasphemed against Him (v.28-30). (Hebrews 6, 10:26-ff)

1st Samuel 2- Sons of Belial.

This chapter presents the plan of God to make a prophet in place of Eli and an eternal priest over His people, who is Jesus Christ.

It begins with the song/ prayer of thanksgiving, praise, and dedication by Hannah for the gift of a son. This prayer is remarkably similar to the Magnificat (Luke 1:46-55) when Mary was praying and praising while pregnant with Jesus. It is an excellent testament to the goodness of God (v1-10): His mercy towards His people, His strengthening and defense of the weak, and His faithfulness to His chosen people, based on His promises in His word.

The focus of our discussion today however will be on the sons of Eli.

"Now the sons of Eli were sons of Belial; they knew not the Lord."-v12

The Bible says that whoever serves the Lord must first believe that He is (an all-powerful, mighty, only true God) and is a rewarder of those who diligently seek Him (faithful, merciful, kind...). Sons of Belial(the devil, sons of rebellion) believe that He is (James 2:19), but they do not seek Him; and the only way to know the Lord is by seeking Him.

They among many things, desecrated the burnt offerings offered unto the Lord, were proud and violent in their behaviour, and had established customs that were contrary to the Levitical order established by God through Moses and this led men (the congregation) to sin by abhorring the sacrifice of the Lord (v.13-17, Ezekiel 22:26, 31).

Eli the high priest heard of his sons' sins and warned them of it to no avail because God had given them over to a reprobate mind (Romans 1:28-32). They committed sexual sins, were rebellious towards God, and were shepherds leading the sheep astray.

Amidst this desert of morality and spirituality we as an oasis in its blooming glory, ***"And the child Samuel grew on, and was in favour both with the Lord and also with men. "(v.26)*** Notice also that this statement is similar to what was said about the child Jesus (Luke 2:52).

Eli received a prophecy from the Lord: reminding him of his sins, his sin of not handling it as the law of God demanded (they were to be stoned according to the law of Moses) but instead seeking their well-being over God's will (v.27-29).

Because of these sins, the Lord has revised the office of the High Priest. Since then, the high priest would be the one who honoured the Lord (v.30-34) and a curse befell Eli's entire house and his sons were to die.

"And I will raise me up a faithful priest, that shall do according to that which is in mine heart and in my mind: and I will build him a sure house: and he shall walk before mine anointed forever." - v35-36.

God appointed Samuel for his office and promised the Messiah to be the hope of the future for His people.

We should cultivate faithfulness and the fear of the Lord in our lives. My prayer is that you will each grow to be the kind of people that God trusts to do His heart and mind; people who honour Him.

Acts 16- Spirit Against Spirit.

Paul was on a mission that lasted his entire life (2nd Timothy 4:6-8). In this chapter, we get to hang out with him on his stopover at Derbe and Lystra, where he met Timothy (who later became a bishop) and took him under his wing. (v.1-5) They did the work together and by their preaching of Jesus, many churches were established in the region and were *"increased in number daily."* (v.5) We also see that his journeys as the apostle to the Gentiles were led by the Holy Ghost (v.6) because when he wanted to go into Asia the Spirit of God forbade them (v.7)

After he had the vision, discerning that the Lord was leading them into Macedonia, they headed there immediately (v.9-10). When they got to Philippi, they met a merchant lady named Lydia, whom the Lord had appointed as their host in that region. Out of the many women present when Paul and his companions spoke, she was the only one who was convicted of Truth and got baptised (v.12-15).

As they were heading off to pray, a certain slave girl possessed with a python spirit (spirit of divination) met them and began proclaiming *" These men are the servants of the Most High God, which shew unto us the way of salvation." (v.17)* Her trade was soothsaying/fortune telling and her master earned off her.

Here, we should note that what the spirit within her was saying was the truth, but she was saying it by the wrong spirit. She was following Paul and his companions around to distract the crowds and rob them of the truth that they were hearing. She followed them around for many days, Paul being frustrated and angered by her antics, *"turned and said to the spirit I command thee in the name of Jesus Christ to come out of her." (v.18)* And he came out the same hour (Philippians 2:9-11).

Let us dwell here awhile and deduce:

- There are other spirits apart from the Holy Spirit that can indwell a human body.

- Spirits are persons/personalities without bodies.

- Prophecy can be uttered from a source other than the Holy Ghost (Charismatic fortune-telling) hence the need to always test the spirit.

- We should exercise and grow our discernment.

- Only a person with the Holy Ghost can tell a fraud.

- The name of Jesus Christ casts out demons.

What followed was a spiritual battle that was played out in the natural.

Paul and Silas were brought before the magistrate by the girl's masters accused of troubling the city by teaching heretic customs (v.19-21) The entire city rose against them and they were undressed, whipped, and thrown into jail (v.22-24).

"At midnight, Paul and Silas prayed and sang praises unto God;" -v.25

All the doors were opened. This occurrence resulted in a win for God's kingdom because the guard ended up being converted (v.26-34). He and all his house believed and were baptised.

Paul and Silas went into jail condemned but came out conquerors because (Romans 8:1) Jesus is the answer to all, ask Him into every area of your life.

He will come in and dwell in you and then He will fill you with the Holy Ghost. And where the Spirit of God is, there is liberty.

2nd Samuel 6- The King of Kings.

After David had smitten the Philistines, *"Again, David gathered together all the chosen men of Israel, thirty thousand."*(v.1)

The men- highly respected, highly honoured, men of valour, men of war, the army of the Lord- were gathered together and led by their king rose early to go and *"bring up from thence the ark of God, whose name is called by the name of the Lord of Hosts that dwelleth between the cherubims."* (v.2)

The ark of God had for a time not been dwelling at the centre around which all Israel pitched tents but had dwelled in Gibeah in the house of Abinadab. It was David's wish- the man who sought God's heart- to bring it back to Jerusalem, and so they set it on a new cart and Abinadab's sons drove the cart (v.3, 4)

It was a joyous occasion and all of David's companions -all the chosen men of Israel- *"played before the Lord"* songs of praise and worship on all manner of instruments (v.5) On their way however, Uzziah committed an abomination by touching the ark of God because he thought it would fall off the cart, there he died (v.6-8).

That happening made David fear the Lord did not want to exacerbate the situation, therefore they carried the ark into the house of Obed-Edom the Gittite (v.9,10) where it dwelled for three months and the Lord blessed the household (v.11-12). This proved to them that the Lord was not angry with the congregation of Israel.

When the news reached David the king he knew that the anger of God had passed and the mercy of God had been restored, therefore he *"went and brought up the ark of God from the household of Obed-edom into the city of David with gladness."* (v.12)

He did it with sacrifices of honour and thanksgiving (v.13), praise, honour, and worship (v.14) -linen ephod was uniform for those in priestly service. This was also a foretelling of the coming of the priestly kingdom (1st Peter 2:9)- with shouting and with the sound of the trumpet (v.15) which was always blown to declare victory.

David danced and leaped before the Lord to the displeasure of his royal wife Michal (v.16), who despised him in her heart.

The ark was placed in the pitched tabernacle and after that, they offered burnt and peace offerings to the Lord (v.17). David blessed the people in the name of the Lord of Hosts (v.18) and also blessed them with physical gifts (v.19). And then it got interesting: (exodus 25:17-18, Leviticus 16:2-39)

IT IS NOT ABOUT ME.

Michal was quick to express her displeasure to the king, calling him vain, inappropriate, and an embarrassment to his estate. (v.20)

David reminded her that he was the king ordained and chosen by the King of kings, he was set to rule over the people whose real Lord was the Lord (v.21). He reminded her that perception and status were less important than worshipping and honouring God. I think, here we begin to understand why David was a man after God's own heart; because to Him, God was FIRST.

Michal never had a child from then (Exodus 20:5,6, Numbers 14:18), the king made it clear that he would lie with a servant girl before touching her ever again.

Psalm 116- Find Rest My Soul.

I love the Lord, he heard my voice and my prayer,
I will call upon Him all my life, for He has lent me His ear;
Death and hell surrounded me, they held me down,
In my deep sorrow, I called "O Lord deliver my soul" when I was struck down,
Gracious is our God, and righteous, yes our God is merciful,
I was brought low and He helped me, The Lord preserves the humble.
Return to your rest oh my soul, the Lord is your place of hiding,
For you have delivered my soul from death, my eyes from tears, and my feet from falling.
I will walk before the Lord in the land of the living.
I believed, therefore have I spoken, while in my great affliction,
I said in my haste, all men are liars.
What shall I render unto the Lord, for all HE has done for me?
I will take the cup of salvation, and call upon the name of the Lord.
I will pay in the presence of all His people my vows unto the Lord.
The death of saints is precious in the sight of the Lord.
O Lord, truly I am thy servant, the son of thine handmaid, thou hast loosed my bonds,
I will offer up the sacrifice of thanksgiving, and call upon the name of the Lord,
I will pay unto the Lord my vows,

In the courts of the Lord's house, in the midst of thee, O Jerusalem, Praise ye The Lord.

All the congregation sing unto the Most High, again and again: for He is good, His mercy endures forever and His faithfulness is to perpetual generations.

(1st Cor.4:20, Col. 1:11, 2nd Cor. 4:7)

2nd Kings 4- Heart Conditions and Systems.

What you believe dictates how you think.

There are four accounts in the life of the prophet Elisha recorded in this chapter, each one in a special way giving us a reason to praise our God in His word. I would however like us to explore them from a different dimension, by looking at the parts that the characters played in the works of the Lord through which His power and might were made manifest. (Ephesians 2:10, Proverbs 4:23).

THE PROPHET'S WIDOW.

The wife of one of the sons of the prophets cried unto Elisha of her due debts to which her sons were collateral (v.1). This gives us a window into the sort of life she and her husband lived, and the heart condition of her husband as the head of the household. They were destitute, living in poverty and borrowing to attain a certain lifestyle. This is a reflection of the spiritual state of Israel at the time, where the people did not give to/for the Lord's work; but it does not excuse their condition. In Deuteronomy 28, the conditions for obtaining God's blessings are fearing and obeying Him. If the prophet's son feared the Lord then his only other malady (even generational malady) was laziness (James 2:17, Proverbs 12:27, 15:19, 18:9, 19:15, 21:25, Matthew 25:26-ff, 26:14,15, Ecclesiastes 10:18).

We are then taught the importance of the helmet of the hope of salvation, because unless she believed she would not have spoken (Psalm 116:10). Then came the golden egg question *"What shall I do for thee?" (v.2)*, to which she answered in a way to show us the substance of her heart (Proverbs 4:23).

"Thine handmaid hath not anything in the house, save a pot of oil." While it is commendable that she was honest, to her a pot of oil counted as nothing. If you believe you have nothing then you are resigned to your sorry state and see yourself as a victim of your circumstances. God, to honour His word, directed Elisha to give instruction *"borrow not few."* He wanted to bless them abundantly. She obeyed, borrowed the vessels, and *"she poured out".* Until her son said *"There is not a vessel more,"* And the oil stopped flowing (v.3-7).- recognize what you have, that is of value, no matter how tiny it is. Then present that to the Lord.

God demonstrated here that He can supply our every need according to His riches in glory, but we have to match by growing in capacity. God's blessing stops flowing when your capacity to contain it is maximised.

THE SHUNAMMITE WOMAN.

This wonderful daughter is described by the Holy Spirit as *"a great woman." (*v.8) Nothing more is said of her character and makeup but I am assuming she was a Proverbs 31 woman because one of her virtues was hospitality and mercy. Every time the prophet Elisha passed that way, he dined in her home. After a while, she convinced her husband to set a room aside where the prophet could board when he travelled through their land. (v.9-11) She was offering kindness and expecting nothing in return, but the Lord was preparing a prophet's reward for her.

One thing is said about her mindset, when asked what she would require of the prophet her answer expressed her contentment with her life (v.12-13).

Gehazi however told his master that she had no child and the prophet promised her a child by the next season, which she got (v.14-17).

Many years, later, the son suddenly fell ill and died, The great woman instead of mourning or complaining, laid up the child in the prophet's room in faith and went and demanded help (v.18-37) She hid it from her husband because she believed in her heart that her son would be made well. ***"It shall be well"*** was her answer to his inquiries.

She went to the prophet in haste, ***"Slack not thy riding for me, except I bid thee."*** Her mindset did not allow for delays and procrastination. When she got to the prophet Elisha, she reminded him that she did not ask for a son, and when she was promised one her only request was not to be deceived. And she said, ***"As my Lord liveth, and my soul liveth, I will not leave thee."*** Do you knock and run off or do you knock until the Lord opens the door? Are you determined and desperate that the Lord should bless you or is it an option for you?

Her son was raised from the dead and she bowed before God and rejoiced.

THE SONS OF THE PROPHETS IN GILGAL.

There was a great famine in the land, and Elisha sent his servant to go and gather whatever he could find so that the sons of the prophets would have something to eat. (v.38-39)

The servant unknowingly cooked poisonous plants, and when the sons of the prophets went to eat, they discovered it and cried out,

"O thou man of God, there is death in the pot."

Can you hear the panic and helplessness in their voices?

And can you hear the peace and trust in Elisha's voice when he said ***"Bring meal"*** And triumph and thanksgiving when he said, ***"Pour out for the people, that they may eat."*** And there was no harm in the pot. Do you trust God that much?

BREAD MULTIPLIED.

It is no wonder that when they received the first fruits from the man from Baalshalisha and there were more hungry men than loaves, Elisha trusted God.

When his servant, a man of fickle faith, asked *"What should I set this before a hundred men?"* He said again, *"Give the people, that they may eat, and shall leave thereof."* According to the word of the Lord, it was so (v.42-44).

Jude - Fight To Keep The Fatih.

Before we begin the exegesis, let me first say that Jude the brother of James could write! His book, only 25 verses long, is a masterpiece!

He began with a salutation

" Jude, the servant of Jesus Christ, and a brother of James, to them that are <u>sanctified by God the Father</u> (Romans 8:29-30), and preserved in Jesus Christ, and <u>called</u> (Romans 8:28); mercy unto; and peace, and love, be multiplied." (v.1, 2)

He wished them the mercy of God that endures forever, the peace from the Son that surpasses all understanding, and the perfect love of God that casts out all fear and covers (red) all faults.

He then proceeded to the main reason for his writing an epistle :
"It was needful for me to write unto you, exhort you that ye should earnestly contend for the faith which was once delivered unto the saints." (v.3) He reminded them to maintain and fight to keep the faith first granted to them through grace by faith.

The true gospel that was untainted, uncorrupted, and spoke of the first love. This is why; certain men crept into the congregation 'unawares', according to Jude were *"ordained to this condemnation"*, according to God had given them up to this deception (sons of Belial); *"ungodly men, turning the grace of our God into lasciviousness and denying the only Lord God, and our Lord Jesus Christ." (v.4)*

These men were using the grace of God as a licence to sin- to live in lewdness, excesses, and feeding their lusts (1st John 2:15-17)- and they also denied that Jesus Christ is Lord. They had the Spirit of antichrist (1st John 2:22).

He proceeded to remind them how God, who is long-suffering and merciful but will not forgive the guilty, dealt with such in the course of history.

How the Lord by His mighty deeds saved the people of Israel out of Egypt but afterward in the desert destroyed all who believed not (v.5).

The angels in heaven who rebelled against God, whom God, whom God had put in everlasting chains under darkness awaiting the judgement of the great day (v.6).

Sodom and Gomorrah and the neighbouring cities, who gave themselves to fornication and went after strange flesh (other forms of sexual immorality), who suffered the vengeance of eternal fire.

He compares the ungodly men to the above three situations; *"Likewise also these filthy dreamers defile the flesh, "like Sodom and Gomorrah... despise dominion" like the fallen angels and "...Speak evil of dignities " (v.8)* like the Israelites in the desert.

Defiling the flesh in the Bible includes; fornication, adultery, bestiality, homosexuality, fleshly lust, sleeping with dead bodies, sodomy, and rape.

Despising dominion is disrespect and dishonour to the established headship of a certain territory, domain, or institution. Finally, speaking evil of dignitaries is insulting the character and acts of those who have authority over you.

He juxtaposes their conduct with that of the archangel Michael, when contending with the devil disputing over the body of Moses, did not accuse him but said *" The Lord rebuke thee," (v.9)* Because the Lord is head over all and Michael understood and respected his assignment, and stayed within its bounds. In contrast, these ungodly men, in their pride and self-will *"Speak evil of those things which they know not" (v.10)*, from worldly teachings, costumes, and prejudice *"...But what they know naturally, as brute beasts, in those things they corrupt themselves."* It's like they have no spiritual eyes to see those that are spiritual matters and no ears to hear those that are spiritual matters, hence they are carnally minded. To be carnally minded is enmity with God, their ways are discussed in the the next verses. They show up at charity feasts and eat and drink up everything meant for the poor and needy, they are clouds without water, carried about by winds -people with no substance, built on quicksand- trees with dead fruits, without fruit, twice dead, plucked up by the roots (John 15).

Raging waves of the sea, foaming out their shame; (v.12) wandering stars to whom is reserved the blackness of darkness forever (v.13)

"And Enoch also, the seventh from Adam, ..." prophesied about it, of the Lord coming with ten thousands of His saints, to judge all, to convince the ungodly of the ungodly deeds that they have ungodly committed, and all their speeches the ungodly have spoken against Him (v.14, 15)

They are ungodly: *"Murmurers, complainers, walking after their own lusts; and their mouth speaketh great swelling words"*, they are boasters and flatterers and are respecters of persons, esteeming people based on their earthly possessions (v.16). He also reminded them that the apostles also spoke on this; that in the last times, there will be mockers of the gospel, walking after their ungodly lusts (v.17, 18) They are evident among the congregation, being sensual and lacking the Holy Spirit (v.19).

A beautiful "BUT" follows:

"But ye, beloved, building up yourselves on your most holy faith, praying in the Holy Ghost." He tells them that now that he has taught them the identity, they should also avoid them and their influence, by building themselves up in their most holy faith, praying in the Spirit (v.20) keeping themselves in the love of God, looking for the mercy of our Lord Jesus unto eternal life. (v.21)

Of some of those have compassion (v.22) and discernment and wisdom: others with fear, pull them out of deception, but hate the deception itself (v.23).

He closes with a prayer salutation, praying that they are kept from falling and they are presented faultless before the presence of his glory with exceeding joy. And finally ends with an exaltation of the Most Holy God, the only wise God our Saviour.

Jude's letter is the litmus test for all spirits and how to deal with the results. Make no mistake, we are at war, you have to know your enemy, and know the weapons of war. Then you can fight with prowess and mastery, only the winners get the prize. (1st Corinthians 8,9, 1st Timothy 4).

Ezra 1- That The Word of The Lord May Be Fulfilled.

The book of Ezra begins where 2nd Chronicles ends: with King Cyrus of Persia proclaiming him wanting to build a house in Jerusalem for the Lord God of heaven. It says *"... That the word of the Lord by the mouth of Jeremiah might be fulfilled, the Lord stirred up the spirit of Cyrus, king of Persia..." (v.1)* The Bible says that the Lord has put His word above all His names (Psalm 148:8, Lamentations 2:17, Daniel 9:12, Luke 4:32) and that His word does not come down and go back to Him without fulfilling its purpose. What's more, He follows His word to ensure that it is fulfilled. When He told Abraham that His offspring would be in bondage/ slavery for 400 years, after the time was up he sent Moses.

So King Cyrus with his spirit stirred put out a proclamation in writing saying: that he wanted to build God a house in Jerusalem, he asked if there were any among the children of Israel who would go up, and that whoever remained behind should give those who were going silver, gold, goods, and beasts, besides the free will offering for the house of God (v.2-4). He was giving the Israelites permission to go and re-establish themselves in their land.

"Then rose up the chief of the fathers of Judah and Benjamin, and the priests, and the Levites, will call them, whose spirit God had raised, to go up to build the house of the Lord which is in Jerusalem." -v.5

The men had been stirred by the Lord, but if they had not in their will risen, the mission would have failed. We need to partner with

God in doing His will and His word, for we are His partners and the ambassadors of Christ here on earth.

All those around them, apart from the free will offering gave them as per the edict of the king vessels of silver and gold (wealth store) to be dedicated to the Lord in service at the temple, goods, and beasts for them to have something to rebuild their lives in terms of sustenance as Jerusalem had been left desolate (2nd Chronicles 36:17-20) and other precious things which they could use to trade for what they needed to rebuild the temple (v.6).

Cyrus the king also restored the vessels of the house of the Lord which Nebuchadnezzar king of Babylon had put in the house of his gods. (v.7) (2nd Chronicles 35:18-22, 36:11-16). King Cyrus numbered them to the prince of Judah (v.8, 9)

- thirty chargers of gold,
- a thousand chargers of silver
- twenty-nine knives,
- thirty gold basons,
- four hundred and ten silver basons,
- and other basons to a thousand (v.10).

The king restored unto them all the vessels that were used for service in the temple: for offering sacrifices, cleansing, holding the water of purification, and others: just as the Lord had directed them when He gave them the pattern of the tabernacle while Israel was still in the wilderness. God had given them another chance.

Philemon - Communicating Your Faith.

In this letter Paul referred to Philemon in the most endearing terms "our dearly beloved" and "fellow labourer"; which is appropriate because only to someone whom you love and trust could you say what Paul said to him next (v.1). And wouldn't you want to be beloved Apphia of fellow-soldier Archippus to the astute and faithful Paul (v.2) who by the way at the time was a prisoner in Rome.

He prayed for grace and peace from God the Father and the Lord Jesus Christ, and as you know how importation works, you cannot give what you do not have (v.3) Paul, while a prisoner was still operating in the grace of God and had the peace that surpasses all understanding. (Philippians 4:5-7)

He also said that he offers thanksgiving prayers on their behalf when he hears of their love and faith towards the Lord Jesus and fellow Christians (v.4, 5).

He highlighted a faith principle that I believe is important to adhere to: you do not need to tell unbelievers about Jesus, you need to show them Jesus in your character and your actions. By their acted-out love and faith towards Jesus and each other, the communication of their faith was being made effectual (v.6, 7), by acknowledging every good thing which is in them in Christ Jesus.

Paul the aged (elder) then went on to the main theme of the letter; to *"Beseech thee son Onesimus, whom I have begotten in my bonds."* *(v.10)* He told Philemon that Onesimus was unprofitable to him, but is now made profitable thanks to the renewal in Christ Jesus he had undergone while under the mentorship of Paul in Rome. Renewal opens the door for reconciliation.

Paul vouched for Onesimus- who left Philemon as a servant but returned as a brother in the faith, who departed for a season that he should return forever- even going as far as pegging his reformation on his reputation. He even asked for forgiveness for any wrongs committed by Onesimus (Luke 23:24, 22:31-32, Matthew 10:24-24).

This is a teacher's responsibility to his disciple, a mentor to his mentee; to cover their wrongs and correct them with love.

Paul also hinted at a reminder at Philemon of him being once a student of his (v.19-21) ***"Having confidence in thy obedience I wrote unto thee."*** Finally, he asks them to continue praying for him that perhaps he will be set free and return to them. (v.22)

Effectual faith is actionable; if it does not impact positively, you are failing in your role as ambassador.

1st Samuel 12- Stand Before The Lord.

On this fateful day, the Israelites had to do something that always put fear in their hearts every time they had to do- They had to do something that scares even me, the thought of it fills me with the feeling of reverence and fear- They had to stand before the Lord! (Genesis 19:27, Exodus 23:17, 28:35, Leviticus 6:7, 10:2, Deuteronomy 6:25, 9:18, Judges 20:23) It is frightening to do because standing before the perfect, holy, beautiful magnificent, all-powerful, King of kings and Lord of hosts, all your faults, shortcomings and human fragility are made more apparent. But let us start from the beginning...

It was on the day of Saul's coronation as king of Israel that the chapter's happenings took place. Samuel began by telling them that as per their request, he had made a king over them (v.1) (1st Samuel 8:5-9,19-22). He then went forth to give an account of his leadership to them as prophet and judge: he had never taken anybody's ox or ass, he had never defrauded or oppressed anyone, or received any bribes. And the people swore on that truth with the Lord as their witness (v.2-5). It was important as a change of guard has to be preceded by the predecessor giving an account of their servanthood. He was handing over the role of judge (1st Samuel 7:15-17) to the newly appointed king.

After this came the topic of our discussion today:

"Now therefore stand still, that I may reason with you before the Lord of all the righteous acts of the Lord, which He did to you and their forefathers." BI-v.7

He reminded them that it was the Lord who sent Moses and Aaron to lead their forefathers out of Egypt after they cried out to Him, and brought them where they dwelled. (8)

When they rebelled against the Lord and chose idols when they fought against their enemies and lost (Deuteronomy 28) ***"And they cried unto the Lord."*** the Lord sent Jerubbaal, Jephthah, and Samuel among others and delivered them (v.9-11).

And then, when they saw Nahash coming against them, they forgot all that the Lord had done for them and demanded a king, ***"When the Lord your God was your king." (v.12)***

Despite their rebellion, the long-suffering God gave them a covenant of blessing in their new kingdom setup: ***"If ye will fear the Lord, and serve Him, and obey His voice, and not rebel against the commandments of the Lord, then shall both ye and also the king that reigneth over you continue following the Lord your God; but if ye will not obey the voice of the Lord, then shall the hand of the Lord against you, as it was against your fathers."***- v.14, 15

Then Samuel asked the Lord for a sign from the Lord to show them that He was angry with their unbelief and rejection of Him; it rained and thundered during the dry season. (v.16-18) The people feared and asked Samuel to pray and repent on their behalf (19). Now the veil is torn, praise Jesus we can each pray! (Hebrews 4:14-16)

And Samuel said unto the people ***"Fear not: ye have done all this wickedness: yet turn not aside from following the Lord but serve the Lord with all your heart."*** (20) Then he explained a truth that we have covered in a previous study: if you turn away from following God you will get lost following vain things. *The reality of the human soul is that we do not have a choice on whether to worship but whom to worship;* choose the right child of God (v.21).

And he told them something else, a beautiful truth ***"For the Lord will not forsake His people for His great name's sake; because it hath pleased the Lord to make you His people."*** (v.22)

And Samuel also promised to never stop praying for them and teaching them the right and good way. (v.23)

His final plea was to ***"Fear the Lord and serve Him in truth with all your heart."*** remembering what great things He had done for them (v.24).

Should they choose to follow wicked ways, then they would perish (v.25). A few quick lessons from this study:

- God demands faithfulness.
- We must worship Him in truth.
- The nature of the old man tends to rebellion.
- Serving God is a choice.
- Our God is merciful.

Are you serving God in truth with all your heart?

Conclusion.

This 40-day word fast, ordained by the Holy Spirit, stands as a divine conduit guiding you toward greater maturity. My earnest prayer is that this devotional has truly enriched your life. May it ignite within you a deeper hunger for the Word, a fervent passion for the things of the Lord, and a heightened dedication to prayer. May you become increasingly attuned to and appreciative of your identity in Christ.

No encounter with Jesus leaves a life unchanged, and I am confident that your journey through this devotional has wrought transformative blessings upon your life. If you're already rejoicing in how far you've come, brace yourself, for the journey ahead holds even greater surprises. The word of the Lord assures us of a trajectory "from glory to glory, from grace to grace, from power to power."

If you haven't yet explored my other devotional study, "Abraham's Seed," I urge you not to delay any longer. It's a journey worth embarking upon, a treasure trove of spiritual insights awaiting your discovery.

<u>"Run with endurance, the race set before you."</u>

About the Author

A curious mind who likes to share her discoveries with the world!
Kenyan by birth,
African by heritage,
Christian by Grace.

9 798224 465101